As the Curtain Rises

on Contemporary British Drama

As the Curtain Rises

On Contemporary
British Drama 1966-1976

Douglas Colby

Rutherford • Madison • Teaneck
Fairleigh Dickinson University Press
London: Associated University Presses

© 1978 by Associated University Presses, Inc.

Associated University Presses, Inc.
Cranbury, New Jersey 08512

Associated University Presses
Magdalen House
136–148 Tooley Street
London SE1 2TT, England

Library of Congress Cataloging in Publication Data

Colby, Douglas, 1954–
    As the curtain rises.

    Bibliography: p.
    1. English drama—20th century—History criticism.
2. Stoppard, Tom.   Rosencrantz and Guildenstern are dead.
3. Hampton, Christopher, 1946–   The philanthropist.
4. Pinter, Harold, 1930–   Old Times. 5. Drama—Technique.
I. Title.
PR736.C57   822'.9'1409   77-92566
ISBN 0-8386-2194-5

PRINTED IN THE UNITED STATES OF AMERICA

To my grandparents

Contents

Acknowledgments   9

Introduction   11

1 "The Game of Coin Tossing": *Rosencrantz and
   Guildenstern Are Dead* by Tom Stoppard   27

2 "An Act of Suicide": *The Philanthropist*
   by Christopher Hampton   47

3 "A Vicious Triangle": *Old Times* by Harold Pinter   75

Selected Bibliography   100

Acknowledgments

I wish to express my appreciation to the following people for their contributions to the writing of this book: Tom Stoppard, Christopher Hampton, Kenneth Tynan, Martin Esslin, Guy Vaesen, and Michael Rudman for their informative interviews and letters; Ian Bevan and Harold Fielding for graciously arranging some of these interviews and supplying me with facts about the British theater; Al Hirschfeld for his charming caricature of Stoppard, Hampton, and Pinter; Martha Swope, John Haynes, and Donald Cooper for the use of their excellent photographs; Barbara Anspach, Andrew Anspach, Charles Abramson, Denise DeNezzo, Peter Poullada, Stuart Samuel, and Beatrice Rehl for their uplifting spirits; Susan Zilber for generously helping me acquire photographic materials; Gerald Roscoe and Daniel Seltzer for their keen editorial assistance;

and most of all,

Kendra Hamilton for her enthusiasm, invaluable suggestions, and kind patience.

I would also like to thank the following for permission to reprint material under copyright:

Associated Book Publishers Ltd for nonexclusive, English-language rights throughout the world excluding the U.S.A. to use extracts from Harold Pinter, *Old Times,* published by Eyre Methuen, © 1971 by H. Pinter Ltd.

Faber and Faber Ltd for extracts from Tom Stoppard, *Rosencrantz and Guildenstern Are Dead* and *The Real Inspector Hound,* and also for extracts from Christopher Hampton, *The Philanthropist.* Reprinted by permission of Faber and Faber Ltd.

Grove Press, Inc. for extracts from Harold Pinter, *Old Times, No Man's Land,* and *The Go-Between,* and from Tom Stoppard, *Rosencrantz and Guildenstern Are Dead* and *The Real Inspector Hound.*

Christopher Hampton for permission to quote from his letter to me of July 26, 1977.

Introduction

Drama is distinct from most other forms of literature in that it communicates visually as well as verbally. What we see on stage is as essential to conveying a play's meaning as what we hear. Physical movement, facial expression, even sets and costumes tell us things that words alone do not and that are necessary to a full comprehension of a play.

The visual metaphor, in particular, is a highly effective and theatrical device used to express ideas through visual means. What is meant by *visual metaphor—metaphor* being a term that is usually applied to a figure of speech—is a concrete image presented onstage which represents something more than itself. It is a picture we actually see with our eyes, rather than imagine with our minds, that suggests or embodies the themes of a play.

The particularities of the visual metaphor vary from one example to the next. A symbolic image can be either static (i.e., the frozen configuration of a group of characters, an immobile setting) or dynamic (i.e., an action that is in the process of being performed, a setting that is constantly changing); it can suggest a single theme or evoke many; it can be incidental

11

or pivotal to an understanding of the entire play.

Throughout the history of theater, often the well-constructed play has planted in its initial incident seeds that later grow into fully developed themes. During the last decade in British drama (1966–76), in which attention has been increasingly paid to histrionic aspects of drama, the inherently theatrical and traditional device of the opening visual metaphor has been widely used as a means of providing those germinal ideas. Throughout this period, an astonishing number of plays have incorporated in the opening scene a visual metaphor intended as a key to the meaning of the whole work. As the curtain rises, a symbolic image is immediately presented which clues us to the themes that will be subsequently explored. Strikingly set up, the opening visual metaphor is firmly established in our minds as a reference point for interpreting the evolving action.

The principal aim of this book is to analyze in depth the use of the opening visual metaphor as the interpretive key to three contemporary British dramas written by three different playwrights during the last decade. The works that have been chosen to illustrate this function are *Rosencrantz and Guildenstern Are Dead* (1967) by Tom Stoppard, *The Philanthropist* (1970) by Christopher Hampton, and *Old Times* (1971) by Harold Pinter. Although these plays are very different from one another both thematically and stylistically, they nonetheless are tied by the use of the opening symbolic image.

These plays have been selected not only because they are prime examples of a particular dramatic technique, but also because they represent, in this critic's estimation, the very best work that has been produced in the British theater during the period considered here. In addition, the authors of these plays are three of the most talented and important dramatists currently writing for the British stage, and the specific plays studied are often viewed as the finest they have yet produced as well as ones that epitomize their work as a whole. Many other plays of distinction were created during these years by such gifted playwrights as David Storey, Simon Gray, Trevor Griffiths, Alan Ayckbourn, Peter Nichols, Peter Shaffer, Anthony Shaffer, Edward Bond, and the late Joe Orton, but it is this writer's contention that the three plays chosen share an inexhaustible richness that renders them the most satisfying in the body of recent modern British drama.

Tom Stoppard (b. July 3, 1937), the first playwright whose work will be considered, began his theatrical career as a critic and emerged as a top British dramatist during the late sixties. He is, above all, an offspring of Theater of the Absurd. Many of the themes that we have come to associate with writers such as Beckett, Ionesco, and Genet (the futility of human action, the search for self-definition, the inability to communicate) also appear in the works of Stoppard. The theme of the futility of human action, for instance, is central in the following: *Albert's Bridge* (1967), about a Sisyphean character who struggles to paint a bridge but never completes his task; *Enter a Free Man* (1968), about an inventor's continuous but unsuccessful attempt to break off permanently from his family (also an allegory of Ireland's failing effort to cut its ties from its mother country, England); *Jumpers* (1972), which revolves around a philosophy professor's unceasing endeavor to prove the existence of God; *Travesties* (1974), in which an aging and forgotten actor tries, to no avail, to make himself important by recalling his "intimate" association with James Joyce, Tristan Tzara (the Dadaist poet), and Lenin during World War I; *Rosencrantz and Guildenstern Are Dead,* in which two minor characters from *Hamlet,* caught up in the play's action, repeat the same movements from one performance to the next and thereby always end up just where they began.

Stylistic components of Theater of the Absurd, notably the lack of realism and the use of exaggerated symbol, also characterize Stoppard's work: *After Magritte* (1970) mirrors in dramatic form the surrealism of a Magritte painting; *Jumpers* includes in its cast of characters eight acrobatic professors of philosophy whose gymnastic stunts onstage broadly symbolize the intellectual feats that they execute offstage; *Rosencrantz and Guildenstern Are Dead* derives all its major themes from another fantastical action, the tossing of a coin and its landing "heads up" ninety-five times in a row.

Although Stoppard is greatly influenced by the Absurdist playwrights, he nevertheless makes the borrowed elements his own, altering and developing them to suit his own dramatic voice. Moreover, he adds to them themes that are more identifiably his (i.e., the dangers of radical liberalism, the function of art) and especially stylistic features that lend the work his personal stamp. The highly intellectualized wit and verbal dexterity of his dialogue—dialogue that dazzles with brilliantly clever puns, epigrams, limericks, and philosophical argumentation—are unmistakably his. Also the intricately woven, maze-like structure of most of his plays could only be the product of Stoppard's cerebral adroitness.

The opening visual metaphor is one more important component especially characteristic of the thoroughly worked out structure of Stoppard's plays. In addition to *Rosencrantz and Guildenstern Are Dead,* which will be discussed in chapter 1, a majority of his other works also utilize this dramatic technique as a striking introduction to theme.

As the curtain rises on the first scene of *Enter a Free Man,* we see the interior of a house, dominated by a portrait of the Queen (before the curtain rises, we also hear "Rule Britannia"). Stoppard thus indicates that this household stands for the established ruling forces of England, forces that he later shows will not release their hold on Ireland, represented by George Riley, the protagonist.

As the curtain rises on the first scene of *The Real Inspector Hound* (1968), a surrealistic play about the experiences of a pair of critics watching a play,[1] we, the audience of Stoppard's

---

1. Like *Rosencrantz and Guildenstern Are Dead,* which is founded upon the incidents in Shakespeare's *Hamlet, The Real Inspector Hound* is built upon the action of another playwright's work. The play-within-a-play being observed by the critics is Agatha Christie's *The Mousetrap,* thinly disguised and fondly parodied. *Travesties,* similarly, revolves around a performance of Oscar Wilde's *The Importance of Being Earnest.*

play, "appear to be confronted by [our] reflection in a huge mirror."[2] An audience that seems to be observing us is seen at the back of the stage. Stoppard here suggests the central theme of the play, the thin line between the worlds on- and offstage, between those of illusion and reality. He most effectively dramatizes this theme later, when the two critics suddenly find themselves onstage and implicated in the play's action, while figures who were previously *dramatis personae* appear out front, situated in the critics' seats and commenting glibly on the play's merits.

At the beginning of *Jumpers,* a mad party is taking place at which a female acrobat, swinging from a chandelier, performs a striptease that culminates in her accidentally crashing into and destroying a tray of glasses.[3] This "provocative" action symbolizes the play's major concern, the intellectual acrobatics being performed by Radical Liberals (the Archbishop of Canterbury, two astronauts, eight professors of philosophy) throughout the topsy-turvy, circus world described in the play —acrobatics that, regrettably, result in the stripping away and ultimate shattering of our romanticism and belief in moral absolutes.

At the beginning of *Travesties,* a polemical play that debates the function of art, James Joyce, Tristan Tzara, and Lenin are seated in three separate sections of a Zurich library during World War I. Their location in three distinct areas symbolizes their representation of three different beliefs about the purpose of art: Tzara's philosophy is "art for art's sake"; Lenin's, "art must serve a social function"; Joyce's, a combination of the two. Their placement in a library, an institution that permanently stores literature and histories, symbolizes the immortality

---

2. Tom Stoppard, *The Real Inspector Hound* (New York: Grove Press, Inc., 1968), p. 7.

3. This striptease actually follows a brief incident in which Dorothy Moore, the protagonist's wife and an ex-musical comedy star, begins to sing a song about the moon but quickly exits after having a nervous collapse. Her belief in the romanticized "Harvest Moon" that she describes in her song has been wrecked by the intellectual acrobatics—subsequently symbolized—of scientists who have just landed two astronauts on the moon and revealed over television the disillusioning barrenness of the lunar landscape.

of these figures whose works will survive the transient horrors of World War I and continue to exert influence on the worlds of art and politics.

As the curtain rises on the first scene of *Dirty Linen* (1976), a light farce concerning sex scandals in British Parliament, Maddie, a tantalizing secretary, surreptitiously enters a deserted meeting room for the House of Commons, removes a pair of sexy French knickers from a bag, and puts them on so that they are hidden underneath her skirt. This act of cautious concealment prefigures the subterfuge of the play's seven members of Parliament who later employ every device they know— including the amusingly forced use of French phrases to maintain a lofty air—to block from view their base escapades with Maddie.

Christopher Hampton (b. January 26, 1946) is something of a phenomenon in the British theater. He has only recently turned thirty and has already had five plays produced in the West End, receiving mostly enthusiastic reviews. His first, *When Did You Last See My Mother?*, was written by the time he was eighteen! All five plays reveal a remarkably talented, versatile, and, to say the least, promising young playwright. One of them, *The Philanthropist,* is the fully realized work of an already mature dramatic voice.

Hampton's plays, unlike Stoppard's, are so totally different from one another in their overall style and content that they defy being categorized into a single school of dramatic writing. *When Did You Last See My Mother?* (1966), about a college student's affair with the mother of his male lover, has the plot of a soap opera. Yet the sensitive writing subdues the tendency toward the melodramatic. *Total Eclipse* (1968) is a historical drama concerning the love-hate relationship between the French Romantic poets Rimbaud and Verlaine, treating the subject in a style that mixes documentary and Romantic elements. *The Philanthropist,* in which the protagonist is a man who seems to like all of humanity indiscriminately, is a contemporary variation of French classical comedy, specifically of Molière's *The Misanthrope*; *Savages* (1973) is a political play revolving around the bombing of an Indian village in Brazil (an incident that actually occurred in 1969) and the related kidnapping of the English diplomat to Brazil (an event that is fictional); *Treats* (1976) is a modish depiction of a love triangle—involving a girl and the two men who compete for her—in London of the mid-1970s.

While Hampton's plays represent five distinct types of drama, there are certain recurring features that link them together as the work of one author. The first is a reference to other creative writers. Hampton, who was a student of literature at Oxford and is now a noted translator of classic and semi-classic dramas (Molière's *Don Juan,* Ibsen's *Hedda Gabler* and *A Doll's House,* Chekhov's *Uncle Vanya,* and Odon Von Horvath's *Tales from the Vienna Woods*), reflects in his own plays a fascination with the private lives, works, and philosophies of such writers.

Total Eclipse not only chronicles the illicit love relationship between the teenage Rimbaud and the middle-aged and married Verlaine, but also explores changes in the artistic and personal lives of the poets once they have separated. Hampton shows that their break-up was followed by a total eclipse—a blocking out of Rimbaud's creative talent and a disintegration of Verlaine's marital as well as overall existence.

The Philanthropist, Hampton's modern-day version of Molière's *The Misanthrope,* closely paraphrases the central philosophical points of the seventeenth-century French comedy. The means of arriving at those conclusions, however, are entertainingly different in the contemporary work, for all the details of character and incident have been turned inside out. Most apparently, the protagonist is now a man who loves, rather than despises, mankind.

A second link between Hampton plays is the appearance of a forceful social or political statement. Hampton is a playwright

acutely aware of crucial issues in the actual world, and he
uses his plays to express his personal beliefs about them and
to exert some influence on his audience.[4] *Savages* is an outcry
against injustices done to the Brazilian Indians. *Treats* encap-
sulates Hampton's own impressions of the emotional and intellectual wasteland of England in the mid-1970s. *The Philanthropist* is a warning about the creeping violence that threatens to
totally demolish an already decaying England. It is noteworthy
that in each of these plays the protagonist is a figure representa-
tive of a whole nation or civilization. Alan West, the English
diplomat in *Savages,* stands for, as his name suggests, Western
civilization and its crimes against the Indians. Ann, the pivotal
member of the love triangle in *Treats,* is characterized by an
"apathy, bewilderment, and sheer wrongheadedness that are
indicative of a more general malaise throughout England."[5]
Philip, the philanthropist, typifies the English people and the
weaknesses that further the decline of the British empire.

A third link between Hampton plays is, of course, the use
of the opening visual metaphor. Hampton, like Stoppard, is
a meticulous craftsman who often uses this particular technique
as an immediate introduction to theme. Three of his plays,
Savages, Treats, and *The Philanthropist,* the last of which will
be studied in chapter 2, include this device as part of their
neatly formed structure.

As the curtain rises on the first scene of *Savages,* our attention it at once drawn to six blazing torches that are being used
as instruments in an Indian ritual celebrating regeneration
and honoring the dead. Hampton thus establishes the Indians'
religious and therefore positive use of fire as an emblem of

---

4. In an interview just prior to the London opening of *Savages,* Hampton
expresses his hope of having some effect on his audience's political awareness,
though he also states his belief that the artist can never drastically alter society:
"I think the theatre wants to have a political influence, but you kid yourself if
you think the work you do is radically going to change the way things happen."
W. Stephen Gilbert, "Hampton's Court," in *Plays and Players,* ed. Peter Ansorge
(London, 1973), p. 36.

5. This quotation is from a letter that Christopher Hampton wrote to the
author on July 26, 1977. Reprinted by permission.

their civilized nature. In the final scene of the play, following the bombing of the Indian village, two white men, who have assisted in the massacre, enter the village and destroy the dead bodies by setting them on fire. The playwright here suggests the drama's principal irony: the white men, who use fire for evil purposes, are the true "savages" in the play, not the Indians.

As the curtain rises on the initial scene of *Treats,* we see the main room of Ann's London flat, the salient feature of which is the sparseness of furnishings. Through the disclosure of this environmental emptiness as well as through the opening dialogue between Ann and one of her lovers, in which the pair is shown to be literally incapable of communicating, Hampton immediately reflects the emotional and intellectual barrenness present in this relationship and, implicitly, in the private lives of people throughout present-day England.

Harold Pinter (b. October 10, 1930), unlike Stoppard or Hampton, was already established during the decade considered here as one of the outstanding dramatists writing for the modern British stage. Several of the plays he had written—most notably *The Birthday Party* (1958), *The Caretaker* (1960), and *The Homecoming* (1965)—had by then been widely accepted as classic contemporary dramas. Pinter himself had earned the reputation of being unique in his field and among the most exciting playwrights in England.

Yet if in this period the playwright himself does not emerge, a new voice within him does, one haunted by the element of time and by the related concepts of memory and the distant past. All the works that he creates during these years (including screenplays based on the novels *The Go-Between* by L. P. Hartley, *Remembrance of Things Past* by Marcel Proust,[6] and *The Last Tycoon* by F. Scott Fitzgerald) center around time-oriented themes, such as the uncertainty of memory, the attempt to recapture the past, time as a spatial landscape, and

---

6. Although Pinter has completed the screenplay for a film based on this work and Joseph Losey has agreed to direct it, the film has not, as of the date of this book's publication, been produced.

the effect of the past on the present through memory.

The theme of the uncertainty of memory, for example, is dominant in the following plays: *Landscape* (1968), in which a middle-aged woman, reminiscing to herself about her youth, recalls one especially pleasurable experience at the beach—an experience that she shared with a man who may have been either her employer or the man now her husband; *Silence* (1969), in which a woman and the two men who have been her lovers deliver separate monologues describing their past relationships—monologues that are contradicted by flashbacks juxtaposed with them; *No Man's Land* (1975), about two elderly British gentlemen who, having met at a bar, return to the house of one of them and try to decide whether or not they have known each other before; *Old Times,* in which a married couple and a female friend from the past expose hidden memories—which may or may not be true—suggesting that a lesbian relationship once existed between the wife and the visitor.

It must be noted that when these new, time-related themes enter into Pinter's work, all the stylistic and thematic components that had defined his work up to this point continue to be vital elements in it. His latest creations are still distinguished by the pauses and silences that punctuate his dialogue with strange meaning; by the unique atmosphere that blends everyday reality with mysterious dreamlike events; and most of all by previous Pinter themes, such as the intruder who threatens present peace and stability, the battle for possession of another individual, sexual ambiguity, and so forth. When, as in *No Man's Land* and *Old Times,* these themes of menace are fused with the poetic and lyrical ones of time and memory, a dramatic tone is created that is altogether new and perhaps even more compelling than that of his previous works.

A structural feature that first appears in his work during this period is the opening visual metaphor. Although all his previous plays had been filled with symbolic content—the blind Negro man in *The Room* (1960), the dumb waiter in *The Dumb Waiter* (1960), the toy drum in *The Birthday Party,* and so forth—none contains an opening symbolic image that serves as a principal conveyor of theme. Now, in *No Man's Land* and *Old Times,* the latter of which is the subject of chapter 3, the opening visual metaphor is incorporated as a key to the meaning of the entire play.

As the curtain rises on the first scene of *No Man's Land,* we see a large and well-furnished room in which heavy curtains cover the windows and the central feature is an "antique cabinet . . . on which stands a great variety of bottles: spirits, aperitifs, beers, etc."[7] Hirst, one of the two main characters, is at the cabinet pouring whiskey. Pinter thus suggests that Hirst, closing the curtains to shut off all contact with the world outside and numbing his brain with alcohol, as he continues to do throughout the play, is a man blocking out all traces of life. As suggested by the name Hirst, which sounds like hearse,[8] he is a man living in an icy and sterile environment, a no-man's-land, on his way to both physical and spiritual death.

In addition to the works of Stoppard, Hampton, and Pinter that contain opening visual metaphors, there is a long list of recent plays by other British authors that include this device. It would be impossible to mention them all, but a few can be cited to demonstrate further the ubiquitous use of these symbolic images throughout the spectrum of dramatic styles.

As the curtain rises on the first scene of David Storey's *The Contractor* (1969), a naturalistic play in which the entire action centers around the putting up and subsequent dismantling of a tent for the wedding of a contractor's daughter, three tent poles are seen, firmly planted in the ground and supported by ropes. Storey thus establishes the play's controlling meta-

---

7. Harold Pinter, *No Man's Land* (London: Methuen, 1975), p. 9.
8. Kenneth Tynan informed the writer in an interview in New York, March 14, 1976 that Hirst and the names of the other characters in the play are also names of English cricketers. Pinter, a great fan of this sport, has in this drama his own private game, using the "cricketers" who battle throughout as his players.

phor: just as a breezy and buoyant tent will be built, founded
upon three main poles, so too a lightly suggestive play of airy
subtext rather than concrete confrontation of theme will be
mounted, based upon a trio of primary concerns—social ten-
sions, as examined in the dealings among the lower-class work-
men who erect the tent, the bourgeois contractor and his family,
and the aristocratic fiancé; familial problems, as explored in the
relationships among three generations in the contractor's household; aesthetic principles, as embodied in the parallel evolution
of the tent and the play, delicate objects of beauty that begin
at a point of nothingness, reach a midpoint of totality, and
terminate in nothingness once more.

Even before the action has begun in Peter Shaffer's *Equus*
(1974), a psychological drama about a youth's blinding of six
horses and a psychiatrist's efforts to cure him of the abnormal
passion that motivated his crime, the curtain is already up,
revealing to the audience out front that another segment of
audience is situated in tiers of seats onstage, arranged in such
a way as to suggest a Greek amphitheater. With this introduction to the staging set up, Shaffer not only prepares us for the
elements of Greek drama within the play—the boy's worship
of the god Equus, the psychiatrist's dreams of sacrificing children to the gods, ritualism in the staging, and so forth—but
also, by having all members of the audience face each other
and by forcing us, through this mirror, to recognize ourselves
as observers of the action rather than participants in it, he
creates a significant tie between ourselves and the psychiatrist,
notably the only character who later directly addresses the
audience. The playwright makes us see that we, like Dr. Dysart,
are only "analysts" of the boy's strange emotions, studying them
at a distance and intrigued by them, but ultimately incapable
of fully understanding, experiencing, and therefore fairly
judging what he feels so intensely.

As the curtain rises on the first scene of Alan Ayckbourn's
Absent Friends (1975), a domestic comedy in which a group

of five friends—two married couples and the female half of another—hold a tea party to console another comrade, whose fiancée has just drowned by accident, we see the modern executive-style living room of one of the couples, cheerfully furnished except for a few "doubtful paintings"[9] conspicuously placed. With the unveiling of this symbolic set design, a large interior space of happiness that frames smaller scenes of sadness and doom,[10] Ayckbourn reminds us of the notion that tragedy often exists within the borders of comedy and vice versa. In this way he anticipates for us the play's ironic twist: the five comforting friends, who would seem to be living in an atmosphere of total contentment, reveal themselves to be a generally miserable lot, owing to the infidelity, ennui, and overall dissatisfaction among them; meanwhile, the visiting friend, whom we expect to be mournful over his recent loss, is utterly mirthful, choosing to find pleasure in the still living memories of happy times spent with his fiancée and his present company.

The opening visual metaphor is only one of many possible starting points for interpreting a play. Yet for a large number of the dramatic works created during the last decade, it proves the most rewarding, for through its passage we are often led to endless, interconnected paths of further revelation. This introduction has pointed out and discussed in brief several examples of this device. The chapters that follow will also explore at length the channels that lead out of these initial symbolic images and toward more complete studies of the entire plays from which they emerge.

---

9. Alan Ayckbourn, *Absent Friends* (London: Samuel French, 1975), p. 1.

10. The specific paintings on view in the 1975 London production designed by Derek Cousins included a brooding portrait of a young girl playing a guitar, calling to mind the deceased fiancée, and a violent picture of a ship in a storm at sea, reminding one of the fiancée's tragic drowning.

As the Curtain Rises

on Contemporary British Drama

1 *"The Game of Coin Tossing":*
Rosencrantz and Guildenstern Are Dead
by Tom Stoppard

Brian Murray and John Wood in the opening scene of *Rosencrantz and Guildenstern Are Dead,* original New York production directed by Derek Goldby, 1967. *Photograph courtesy of Martha Swope.*

*A*s the curtain rises on the first scene of Tom Stoppard's
Rosencrantz and Guildenstern Are Dead, the two title
characters are passing the time by betting on the toss of a coin.
Waiting in Elsinore to be summoned by the king and having
nothing better to do, these Elizabethan courtiers engage in a
bit of friendly gambling. Rosencrantz, apparently, is already
winning: his money bag is virtually full, while his companion's
is nearly empty. Furthermore, as the action continues, it soon
becomes evident that he is not about to lose. Every time that
Guildenstern tosses a coin, Rosencrantz guesses "heads" and
without fail proves to be correct. In total, he is right ninety-
five times, a number that seems impossible. Despite the law
of probability, not a single coin lands "tails up."

In this, the opening scene of the play, Stoppard presents
a multileveled visual metaphor that encompasses the four major
themes of the play. The tossing of a coin and the resulting
run of "heads" is a symbolic action that introduces the ideas
that the rest of the play develops.

The first of these themes, which stems from the idea that
there are two sides to every coin, is that there are also two
sides to the story of Rosencrantz and Guildenstern. That is,
the two existing plays which tell the history of the two courtiers[1] tell it from perspectives that are the reverse of each other.

---

1. In addition to the full-length plays *Hamlet* and *Rosencrantz and Guildenstern
Are Dead,* there is a short burlesque titled *Rosencrantz and Guildenstern* that
records events in the lives of the two courtiers. Written by W. S. Gilbert of
Gilbert and Sullivan, it was first produced on June 3, 1891, in London.

In *Hamlet* the action focuses on the prince of Denmark, Claudius, Gertrude, Horatio, and so forth; Rosencrantz and Guildenstern are only minor characters whose story is unraveled incidentally, when they cross the paths of the central characters and thereby step into the unfolding plot. In contrast, in *Rosencrantz and Guildenstern Are Dead* the action spotlights the two courtiers; Hamlet, Claudius, Gertrude, Horatio, et al. are now the peripheral figures whose story is told in passing. In Shakespeare's play Rosencrantz and Guildenstern are insignificant pawns in Claudius and Hamlet's great game of political intrigue, while in Stoppard's they are "important" characters in their own right.

Stoppard reinforces the idea that his play (meaning that part of the play he has written, therefore excluding the scenes he has borrowed from *Hamlet*) is the reverse side of Shakespeare's by employing an intricate symbolic device. He uses the appearance of opposite sides of the coin to point out that dramas which are flip sides of each other are being juxtaposed in *Rosencrantz and Guildenstern Are Dead*. At the beginning of the play, when Stoppard's material is being performed, Guildenstern tosses only "heads": one side of the coin appears in conjunction with the acting out of a single author's work. Just as a scene from *Hamlet* is about to be staged, however, Rosencrantz, replacing Guildenstern as tosser, flips a coin that lands "tails up": the appearance of the other side of the coin signals that *Hamlet,* the flip side of *Rosencrantz* and *Guildenstern Are Dead,* is about to be performed.

Not only is Stoppard's play the reverse side of Shakespeare's, but also it is the complementary one: it is the missing half that completes the whole Elizabethan tale. When Stoppard interpolates speeches from *Hamlet* into the action of his own play, he often attaches additional meanings to them. Such a speech is that delivered by Claudius upon his becoming suspicious of the Danish prince's recent change in character.

> Something have you heard
> Of Hamlet's transformation, so call it,
> Sith neither th' exterior nor the inward man
> Resembles that it was.[2]

In the context of *Hamlet,* "exterior" versus "inward" man describes the Danish prince's physical appearance as distinquished from his inner feelings. In *Rosencrantz and Gildenstern Are Dead,* however, these terms also refer to his visible versus his hidden existence. We are made aware that dramatic characters lead two lives, one which the playwright shows us in his work, the other which he lets remain unseen. That of the "exterior" man is presented for viewing before the audience. That of the "inward" man, undramatized, goes unrecognized by us. It is known to the character alone, in his inner mind.

The reference to these different existences is made not so much to explain the condition of Hamlet as to cue us that Rosencrantz and Guildenstern have a life outside the negligible one that Shakespeare presents. They continue to exist even after they have completed their scenes in *Hamlet* and exited from Shakespeare's world. In his own play Stoppard displays this other life and thereby supplies the complementary half of the courtiers' total existence. He presents a world on the other side of the looking glass, in which Rosencrantz and Guildenstern "do on stage the things that are supposed to happen off. Which is a kind of integrity, if you look on every exit as being an entrance somewhere else" (p. 28).

It must be noted that by writing his play and making this complementary existence visible to an audience, Stoppard renders that previously "interior" existence "exterior." Consequently, the life of the two courtiers shown in *Hamlet*—a life which is the reverse of that portrayed in *Rosencrantz and Guildenstern*

---

2. Tom Stoppard, *Rosencrantz and Guildenstern Are Dead* (New York: Grove Press, Inc., 1968), pp. 35–36. Page references in the text refer to this edition.

Are Dead—necessarily becomes "interior." Stoppard underscores this new order with another symbolic device. When his
own scenes are being performed, he uses lighting to create the
atmosphere of an exterior. However, when these scenes end
and Shakespearean ones begin, *"a lighting change sufficient to
alter the exterior mood into interior"* (p. 34) takes place.

The second theme introduced in the opening visual metaphor—a theme that is also suggested by the two-sidedness of
a coin—is that Rosencrantz and Guildenstern are essentially
two sides of the same person. Because they are only minor
characters in *Hamlet,* included primarily as a tool to forward
the plot, Shakespeare has spent little time developing and differ-
entiating their characters. They are granted only intermittent
involvement in the play's action

> ROS: Incidents! All we get is incidents! Dear God, is it too
> much to expect a little sustained action?! (P. 118)

and a single voice through which to speak: their lines emerge
from the linked pair, not from separate individuals.

> ROS: Both your majesties
> Might, by the sovereign power you have
>   of *us*,
> Put your dread pleasures more into command
> Than to entreaty.
> GUIL: But *we both* obey,
> And here give up *ourselves* in the full bent
> To lay *our* service freely at your feet,
> To be commanded.
>   (P. 36; emphasis added)

As a result, these sadly neglected *dramatis personae* are virtually
indistinguishable from each other. We, the audience, have
trouble discriminating between the two, and so do characters
within the play:

KING: Thanks, Rosencrantz and gentle Guildenstern.
QUEEN: Thanks, Guildenstern and gentle Rosencrantz.
(Pp. 36–37)

From each perspective, the two characters function as a single
identity, the boyhood friend of Hamlet who is commissioned to
escort the Danish prince to England.

In *Rosencrantz and Guildenstern Are Dead,* Stoppard maintains the integrity of Shakespeare's minimally drawn character-
izations. The two courtiers are again like Tweedle Dee and
Tweedle Dum, twin characters who seem to be identical and
also add up to only one identity. As Stoppard comically reveals,
Rosencrantz himself has great difficulty distinguishing between
himself and his companion.

ROS: My name is Guildenstern, and this is Rosencrantz.
(GUIL *confers briefly with him.*)
(*Without embarrassment.*) I'm sorry—*his* name's Guilden-
stern and *I'm* Rosencrantz. (P. 22)

Here too they are a tied pair who speak as one: much of the
dialogue between them consists of lines that flow into each
other as if originating from one source.

ROS: He's the player.
GUIL: His play offended the King—
ROS: —offended the King—
GUIL: —who orders his arrest—
ROS: —orders his arrest—
GUIL: —so he escapes to England—
ROS: —On the boat to which he meets—
GUIL: —Guildenstern and Rosencrantz taking Hamlet—
ROS: —who also offended the King—
GUIL: —and killed the King—
ROS: —and killed Polonius—
GUIL: —offended the King in a variety of ways—

ROS: —to England. (*Pause.*) That seems to be it. (P. 117)

While the two courtiers are uncannily similar, however, they are also notably different. It is true that they are two sides of the same coin, but just as "heads" and "tails" are distinct from each other, so too are Stoppard's versions of Rosencrantz and Guildenstern. Guildenstern, who tosses only "heads," is characterized as the brains. Rosencrantz, who flips only "tails," is marked the ass.

This polarity is illustrated first by Guildenstern's success and Rosencrantz's failure at correctly identifying which courtier is which. It is delineated secondly by the characters' contrasting responses to their coin tossing. Guildenstern, recognizing that the phenomenal results of their gambling must have some great implication for them, systematically and logically examines several possible explanations.

GUIL: It must be indicative of something, besides the redistribution of wealth. (*He muses.*) List of possible explanations. One: I'm willing it. Inside where nothing shows, I am the essence of a man spinning double-headed coins, and betting against himself in private atonement for an unremembered past. . . .

Two: time has stopped dead, and the single experience of one coin being spun once has been repeated ninety times. . . . On the whole, doubtful. Three: divine intervention, that is to say, a good turn from above concerning me, cf. children of Israel, or retribution from above concerning me, cf. Lot's wife. Four: a spectacular vindication of the principle that each individual coin spun individually . . . is as likely to come down, heads as tails and therefore should cause no surprise each individual time it does. (P. 16)

Rosencrantz, on the other hand, acts like a fool when he tries to assist in the investigation. All he can do to help is cite totally irrelevant and absurd information about the growth of fingernails and beards during life and death.

> ROS: (*cutting his fingernails*): Another curious scientific phenomenon is the fact that the fingernails grow after death, as does the beard.
> . . . The fingernails also grow before birth, though *not* the beard. (P. 18)

Throughout their ardent pursuit of answers that will make sense of their situation, the thinking Guildenstern with his proposal of cogent theories is always "ahead," while the mindless Rosencrantz with his inane mimicing or attempts at substantiation of these theories is forever "behind."

> GUIL (*turning on him furiously*): Why don't you say anything original! No wonder the whole thing is so stagnant! You don't take me up on anything—you just repeat it in a different order.
> ROS: I can't think of anything original. I'm only good in support. (P. 104)

The third theme introduced in the opening visual metaphor stems from the reality that Guildenstern's consistent tossing of "heads" is more than the result of luck. Ninety-five "heads" in a row, a more than unlikely event under the law of probability, can only be the product of fate. Similarly, all the other experiences that Rosencrantz and Guildenstern undergo are predetermined, predetermined by Shakespeare and Stoppard. One of the central ideas in *Rosencrantz and Guildenstern Are Dead* is that characters in any play are predestined by its author. From the moment it begins until the last scene is ended, that play can head in only one direction, the one prescribed by the script. The characters, who are swept along by the plot, have no free will. The playwright has chosen a course for them, and they are forced to follow it.

> ROS: We've been caught up. Your smallest action sets off another somewhere else, and is set off by it. Keep an eye open, an ear cocked. Tread warily, follow instructions. . . . There's a logic at work—it's all done for you. (Pp. 39–40)

Therefore, as Shakespeare and Stoppard dictate in the texts of their plays: the two attendant lords will be summoned to the king's court, given orders to accompany the prince of Denmark to England, and ultimately be executed upon delivering the letter that seals their death. Their end is fixed from the very moment either play begins, and they have no power to evade it.

> ROS: They had it in for us, didn't they?
> Right from the beginning.
>
> (P. 122)

From Shakespeare and Stoppard's viewpoints, Rosencrantz and Guildenstern are little more than their own, not just Claudius and Hamlet's, private game, for the two courtiers are only chess pieces they take pleasure in maneuvering and, in another sense, victims of the deadly fate they have chosen to hunt them down.

> GUIL (*musing*): The law of probability, it has been oddly asserted, is something to do with the proposition that if six monkeys (*he has surprised himself*) . . . if six monkeys were . . .
> ROS: Game?
> GUIL: Were they?
> ROS: Are you?
> GUIL (*understanding*): Game. (Pp. 12–13)

Although Rosencrantz and Guildenstern are fated to die

during both *Hamlet* and *Rosencrantz and Guildenstern Are Dead,* they are also set to be reborn as soon as either of these plays begins to be performed again. The life of a play is cyclical in that the end of one performance leads into the beginning of another; the characters involved in the play repeat the same actions from one performance to the next.

> GUIL: . . . we are brought round *full circle* to *face again* the single *immutable* fact—that we, Rosencrantz and Guildenstern, bearing a letter from one king to another, are taking Hamlet to England. (P. 101; emphasis added)

Therefore, although the two courtiers expire temporarily by the end of each play, overall they are immortal, for they continue to come alive after every death. Following every execution and a brief nonexistence in between performances, they are reborn —when the same man, who has always done so, once again awakens them from death to let them begin their lives once more.

> GUIL: Practically starting from scratch. . . . An awakening, a man standing on his saddle to bang on the shutters, our names shouted in a certain dawn, a message, a summons. (P. 20)

One important device that Stoppard uses in his play is to have his protagonists not only encounter their destiny, but also recognize that it exists. He lets them temporarily step outside themselves and their worlds to see objectively that they are caught up in the wheel of fate (which for them is the action of a play) and that they cannot extricate themselves from its centrifugal force.

> GUIL: Wheels have been set in motion, and they have their own pace, to which we are . . . condemned. Each move is dictated by the previous one—that is the meaning of order. (P. 60)

They know that they have lived and died before, during past performances,

> GUIL: And it *has* all happened. Hasn't it? (P. 108)

> ROS: [Hamlet] murdered us. (P. 56)

that they are headed toward death in the present one,

> ROS: It's all heading to a dead stop. (P. 38)

and that they are forever doomed to replay the same scenes in future performances.

> GUIL: We move idly towards eternity, without possibility of reprieve or hope of explanation. (P. 121)

Because Rosencrantz and Guildenstern realize that they are to be "resurrected" in the next performance, they are also aware that corporeal death for them is not really tragic. Even at the climax of the play, as they are about to be executed, they are looking forward to their next life, facing their approaching death calmly.

> GUIL: Well, we'll know better next time. Now you see me, now you—(*and disappears*). (P. 126)

However, because Rosencrantz and Guildenstern also recognize that they lack free will, they see that they are in a perpetual state of spiritual death—a state that is genuinely tragic because there is no possibility of escape. That they themselves consider their inability to control their actions a form of spiritual death is most clearly revealed in the last act of the play. Rosencrantz and Guildenstern are on a boat that transports them and Hamlet to England. Although the two courtiers can move around as they wish within the confines of the moving vessel, they have no choice in determining their final destination. The boat, which is carrying them inexorably toward their execution, represents fate—a fact that Guildenstern himself recognizes.

> GUIL: Free to move, speak, extemporize, and yet. We have not been cut loose. Our truancy is defined by one star, and our drift represents merely a slight change of angle to it: We may seize the moment, toss it around while the moments pass, a short dash here, an exploration there, but we are brought round full circle to face again the single immutable fact—that we, Rosencrantz and Guildenstern, bearing a letter from one king to another, are taking Hamlet to England. (P. 101)

On the boat, they "toss a moment" as they would a coin, hoping that any outcome is possible. Yet they hope in vain, for just as their coin can end up landing on only one side, so too their time spent on the vessel can result in only one conclusion.[3]

In addition to Guildenstern's coming to his realization, Rosencrantz recognizes that the boat also represents spiritual death. When he asks: "Do you think death could possibly be a boat?" (p. 108), he refers not only to his feeling that the boat, which carries them toward the hangman's noose, is the agent of physical death, but also to his sense that to be on the boat and lack free will is to be a hollow puppet controlled by the strings of external forces and therefore spiritually dead.

Finally, by associating both fate and spiritual death with

---

3. Stoppard creates an even stronger connection between the fated courtiers and the predestined coins they toss by subtly revealing that these coins are probably guilders, a word that shares the same root as *Guildenstern* and, by association, objects that share a similar life. The playwright never explicitly indicates that this is the type of change they flip, but he does imply, through the disclosure that it costs ten guilders to see a performance by the traveling tragedians (p. 24), that guilders were widely used medieval currency and therefore likely to be the coins with which they gamble.

the boat, the courtiers, together, implicitly link the two as well. They, as one identity, realize that because they lack free will, Rosencrantz and Guildenstern are dead.

Given the horrifying prospect of not only being in, but also knowing that they are in, a state of living death, Rosencrantz and Guildenstern would seem to be characters existing in a perpetual hell. Yet this is not the case. Stoppard has given them a defense mechanism that turns what would otherwise be a totally tragic existence into one that is half-tragic, half-comic. He lets them partially block from their minds the reality of their condition so that they are only semi-conscious of it. The result is that for them and for us the dark element of their existence is considerably lightened.

This delicate balance between awareness and ignorance is evidenced in the series of double entendres throughout the play. These remarks (unrecognized as two-sided by the courtiers) emphasize that Rosencrantz and Guildenstern view their situation from two separate perspectives, perspectives that work together to create an overall vision that is uncertain.

> ROS: "Question and answer" . . . Hamlet was scoring off us, all down the line. . . . He murdered us. (P. 56)

From one angle, Rosencrantz remembers that Hamlet slaughtered them in a game of question and answer; from the other, he recalls that the Danish prince was responsible for their death in the previous performance.

> ROS: They'll have us hanging about till we're dead. (P. 93)

Rosencrantz complains that for two attendant lords, they have very little attending to do; he also foresees that they will soon be dangling lifelessly from the gallows.

> ROS: Incidents! All we get is incidents! Dear God, is it

too much to expect a little sustained action?! (P. 118)

Rosencrantz again laments the sporadic nature of his work at the court; he also questions Shakespeare, the source of his creation and therefore his God, as to why he and Guildenstern were not blessed with a more constant existence in *Hamlet*.

GUIL: We must have gone north, of course. (P. 99)

Guildenstern remarks that their boat, clearly, has digressed and is currently heading northward; he presumes that it is moving in that direction because that is the course that fate has assigned to them.

This dual vision is what ultimately lets the courtiers maintain their sanity as they are eternally propelled through the two plays. Whenever they face an approaching death, they calm themselves by leaning toward an awareness of being immortal and having a next performance.

GUIL: Well, we'll know better next time. (P. 126)

Whenever they realize that they are immortal only because they are characters in a play, who are also spiritually dead, they sway back to a belief that they are everyday people who have free will.

ROS: We'll be free . . . anything could happen yet. (P. 95)

Guildenstern himself points out in the following epigram the crucial importance of their dual vision:

A Chinaman of the T'ang Dynasty—and, by which definition, a philosopher—dreamed he was a butterfly, and from that moment he was never quite sure that he was not a butterfly dreaming it was a Chinese philosopher. Envy him;

in his two-fold security. (P. 60)

Like the Chinese philosopher, Rosencrantz and Guildenstern are to be envied for being able to see themselves from two different perspectives and never knowing for certain which is the correct one. Their dual vision, like his, is a "two-fold security," for it lets them vacillate between different awarenesses that help them survive emotionally from one moment to the next.

The fourth theme, which again arises from the notion that there are two sides to every coin, concerns two more complementary sides of the two courtiers. Both are characters in a play and also spectators of another play: they are *dramatis personae* in *Hamlet* and *Rosencrantz and Guildenstern Are Dead* as well as the audience watching the drama performed by the traveling tragedians. At one point the Player remarks: "For some of us it is performance, for others, patronage. They are two sides of the same coin" (p. 23). For Rosencrantz and Guildenstern, however, it is both.

Significantly, the dual role-playing of the two courtiers has implications that extend beyond the world of the drama. Their double identity indirectly suggests that we, the audience of Stoppard's play, are also characters in some all-encompassing, cosmic drama. Indeed, if we analyze the different relationships that Stoppard sets up between audience and dramatic character, we eventually arrive at this conclusion: the characters in the play-within-a-play (that of the tragedians) are being watched by Rosencrantz and Guildenstern, the spectators; Rosencrantz and Guildenstern, in turn, are characters in a play who are being watched by us, the audience; we, in turn, are *dramatis personae* in a larger drama.

Not only does Stoppard suggest this idea through the structure of his play, but also Guildenstern implies it verbally. At one point, after the courtier has stated that "Wheels [symbolic of plays and their cyclical course] have been set in motion" (p.

60), he further remarks that "there are wheels within wheels, etcetera" (p. 110). In addition to the fact that one play is being performed over and over again, it is also true that that play is one of an infinite number of concentric plays, all of which repeat themselves endlessly. We, the audience of one of them, are characters in another.

Stoppard, perhaps realizing that our immediate reaction to his idea is to dismiss it as intriguing in theory but farfetched in reality, playfully bombards us with an additional argument, intended to make us reconsider his proposition. In the play performed by the tragedians, there are two characters who are mirror images of Rosencrantz and Guildenstern (in fact, the entire drama that the tragedians act out is a reflection of *Hamlet*). The two courtiers, however, fail to recognize themselves in their counterparts. Although here art mirrors reality, they do not see that it does.

> . . . *under their cloaks the two* SPIES *are wearing coats identical to those worn by* ROS *and* GUIL, *whose coats are now covered by their cloaks.* ROS *approaches "his"* SPY *doubtfully. He does not quite understand why the coats are familiar.* ROS *stands close, touches the coat, thoughtfully . . .*
> ROS: Well, if it isn't—! No, wait a minute, don't tell me— it's a long time since—where was it? Ah, this is taking me back to—when was it? I know you, don't I? I never forget a face—(*he looks into the spy's face*) . . . not that I know yours, that is. For a moment I thought— no, I don't know you, do I? (P. 82)

If we, like Rosencrantz and Guildenstern, reject the proposition that we are dramatic characters as well as spectators, then we too fail to recognize that art mirrors reality. We are as impervious to the truth as the two courtiers.

The first three themes introduced by the opening visual metaphor are all concerned with the nature of drama and dramatic characters. These ideas do not, by themselves, relate to the actual world. However, when they are associated with the fourth theme—that we are all characters in a play—they suddenly pertain to our own condition. If we are characters in a play, then all the aspects that the first three themes attribute to *dramatis personae* should also be applicable to ourselves. First, in some unknown sphere, the history of our lives is being told in a drama that is the reverse and complement of the one we are in. Secondly, everyone in "our drama" may be one of two sides of the same person. Thirdly and most importantly, we, being characters in a play, have all our actions predetermined for us by fate.

Not only does the play's structure inform us of this last reality, but Rosencrantz and Guildenstern do as well. Throughout the drama, we, the audience that includes Stoppard, sit back and analyze from a safely removed distance the semitragic state of the two courtiers. In one brief, but triumphant moment, however, Rosencrantz and Guildenstern have their opportunity to retaliate and tell us that we are predestined too. In the opening, coin-tossing scene, the two courtiers engage in another conversation that has two levels of meaning.

> GUIL: (*flipping a coin*): There is an art to the building up of suspense.
> ROS: Heads.
> GUIL: (*flipping another*): Though it can be done by luck alone.
> ROS: Heads.
> GUIL: If that's the word I'm after. (P. 12)

On one level, Rosencrantz and Guildenstern delight in their ability to create tension as they toss one coin after the other and anticipate results. On the other, they, peering out into our world, tell Stoppard tnat his playwrighting is controlled by the forces of predestination. His "art to the building up of suspense" is not an endeavor that he undertakes out of his own free will. Rather, it is one forced upon him by "fate," the word they constantly search for as the correct substitute for "luck."

We in the actual world, as represented by Stoppard, are predestined in every step we take. Although we seem to have free will, the appearance of our having control over ourselves is only an illusion. Like Rosencrantz and Guildenstern, we are characters caught up in a drama, doomed to replay the same scenes and therefore relive the same lives over and over again. We too, condemned to the wheel of fate, are spiritually dead.

2 "*An Act of Suicide*": The Philanthropist by Christopher Hampton

Andrew Neil in the opening scene of *The Philanthropist,*
original London production directed by Robert Kidd, 1970.
Photograph courtesy of John Haynes.

A s the curtain rises on the first scene of *The Philanthropist,*
Christopher Hampton, the author, plays a trick on the
audience. Three characters are onstage in the bachelor apartment of Philip, a university professor. Philip and Don, his
fellow teacher, are listening attentively to John, a young man
who is holding a revolver and threatening to commit suicide.
John is not merely toying with the professors for effect. Not
only do his words insist that he is sincere,

> JOHN: You needn't think I'm not serious. Because I am.
> I assure you I am.[1]

but most importantly, when he asks rhetorically whether or not
his intention is manifest,

> JOHN: Can't you see that? (P. 9)

all visible evidence—his determined grasp on the gun and his
frenzied manner—affirm positively that he is set on blowing
his brains out.

Philip and Don have hurt John in some way that is undis-
closed to us, and John is resigned to getting even with them.
He plans to kill himself in front of them and let them know
that they are responsible for his action, thereby leaving them

1. Christopher Hampton, *The Philanthropist* (London: Faber and Faber, 1970),
p. 9. Page references in the text are all to this edition.

49

with a visual impression of his gruesome death to haunt them with guilt for the rest of their lives.

> JOHN: I've come here this evening because I think both of you are responsible for this and I think you deserve it as much as I do. If you hate me for doing it, that's your problem. It won't concern me. *I just want you to have one vivid image of me, that's all, one memory to last all your life and never vanish,* to remind you that if you won, I lost, and that nobody can win without somebody losing. (P. 9; emphasis added)

Hopelessly bent on his course of revenge, John takes the final steps toward self-annihilation. He says his last goodbye . . . puts the revolver to his head . . . and says "Bang . . . Curtain."

John is a playwright, and all this time he has been reading an excerpt from his new drama. He has come to the professors for honest criticism and professional advice. Never has he even considered killing himself. Philip and Don have known all the while that he is acting, but we, the audience of Hampton's play, have been duped into believing that he is truly suicidal. Hampton has set up an elaborate visual lie calculated to mislead us, and we have been easy prey to its every ingredient. John's hold of a lethal weapon and enraged manner, his address to *two* people ("both of you are responsible for this"), who could easily be the pair of professors we view before us, and his emphasis that everything we see is real have, together, successfully served the purpose of deceiving us.

With the presentation of the opening visual metaphor, John's apparent suicide, Hampton warns us that in the world of his play, things are seldom what they seem. We are entering territory in which appearances belie reality, and we must take heed not to be fooled by them. Actions, speeches, and especially characters are to be studied cautiously, for they may prove to be contrary to our original conceptions of them. Indeed, during the course of the play we shall make several more surprising discoveries, the first of which is that all the remaining characters in this work are also "role-players" who deceive, or they are those deceived, or they are both.

Philip, the play's protagonist, is chief among the deceived. He, of all its characters, is the most easily gulled because he suffers from one overriding flaw—a chronic inclination to see only surfaces, not what lies beneath. This tendency shows in his response to both words and people. As suggested by his name, Philip is a philologist and philanthropist—a lover (*phile*) of language and mankind, who finds something to like in every word and person. Unfortunately and unadmirably, he loves them both superficially, appreciating only surface aspects of their beauty.

The shallowness of Philip's love of language reveals itself in the confinement of that love to word games such as anagrams. He is obsessed with scrambling and unscrambling letters to form new sentences, but he is basically indifferent to the meaning of connected ones. He does refer to a dictionary when definitions of individual words are useful to him in his useless solving of puzzles, but he is not concerned with the larger and more significant meanings that the joining of words produces. In short, the content of sentences, paragraphs, and ultimately literature eludes him.

> PHILIP: I'm fascinated by words.
> JOHN: Individual rather than consecutive.
> PHILIP: Yes. My only advice to writers is "make the real shapes."
> JOHN: Pardon?
> PHILIP: It's an anagram of "Shakespeare" and "Hamlet."
> (Pp. 11–12)

Because Philip's interest lies in form ("making shapes") rather than content, Shakespeare and Hamlet are important to him only as words whose letters can be rearranged to create a new phrase.

As a consequence of his perceptual limitations, Philip is unable to give John a fair appraisal of his play. First, he does not fully comprehend the work, for he is too literal-minded to discern its allegorical content. For example, although it is clear that the window-cleaner character named "Man" stands for everyman, Philip thinks "he was just meant to represent a window cleaner." (p. 11). Secondly, Philip, who likes all words and therefore all literature indiscriminately, necessarily admires John's play too, despite its obvious amateurishness.

> PHILIP: I always like things. I get pleasure from the words that are used, whatever the subject is. I've enjoyed every book I've ever read, for one reason or another. That's why I can't teach literature. I have no critical faculties. (P. 12)

The superficiality of Philip's passion for words, a serious fault in itself, is also significant as a symptom of his far graver weakness, the shallowness of his love of people. Philip is able to like everyone, and thus qualify as a philanthropist, because he views people on the same surface level as he does words. Just as he fails to see the deeper meanings of language, he is blind to the hidden frailties of people that lie beneath the outer veneer of goodness. Even when these weaknesses are blatantly apparent, he ignores them and focuses instead on any trace of virtue he can find.

> PHILIP: I think there's always something good to be found in the product of another man's mind. Even if the man is, by all objective standards, a complete fool. (P. 12)

Philip's willingness to overlook these shortcomings is rooted not so much in his generosity of spirit as in his lack of moral convictions. Although he himself seems to be a perfectly up-right individual, he has no firm opinions about what others should or should not be or, for that matter, what good and bad are. As Hampton comically reveals, Philip is not even certain that he is certain about nothing.

> PHILIP: My trouble is, I'm a man of no convictions. (*Longish pause.*) At least, I think I am. (CELIA *starts laughing.*) (P. 55)

Morally spineless, he is a glob of shakey gelatin bending with approval to every person he meets.

> CELIA: You're so incredibly . . . bland. You just sit there like a pudding, wobbling gently. (P. 53)

The danger inherent in Philip's automatic acceptance of everyone is that it prevents him from reaching an accurate understanding of anyone. Because he never stops to consider both the positive and negative aspects of people, he cannot possibly assess their true characters. This inability to know who and what people really are is most stingingly examined in his failure to see even into the mind of Celia, his fiancée and most intimate acquaintance. When she speaks to him, he listens to what she says but understands only the literal meaning of her words, not the thoughts and certainly not the feelings behind them. Partly because he is literal-minded, but mostly because he has no sense of Celia's inner nature, he cannot grasp the spirit of her statements.

> CELIA: You never understand what I'm trying to say.
> PHILIP: Maybe not, but I think I usually understand what you do say. (P. 55)

Most dangerously, Philip's ignorance of people's true character makes him a likely prospect to be deceived by them. His "friends" merely have to assume false identities, and he, unable to detect the playing of roles, will take it for granted that they

are projecting their real selves. Such masquerading, as Philip
eventually discovers, is exactly what has been taking place all
around him; for during the course of the play, he learns through
an alarming procession of unmaskings that none of the people
in his life is what he or she has seemed to be. One by one, each
removes his disguise and reveals a markedly different person
behind it.

Araminta, one of the guests at Philip's dinner party, appears
to Philip, despite warnings, to be an intellectual interested in
him mainly because of their mutual love of words.

> PHILIP: She's one of the few people I come into contact
> with who has any interest in my subject at all. She
> seems quite intelligent, so I asked her [to the
> party]. (P. 16)

Therefore, at the end of the evening, when she asks to stay
and clean up, he accepts her offer, thinking it is both innocent
and generous. Upon the departure of the other guests, however,
he is shocked to learn that she is actually interested in him
primarily for sex. She is not the sweet and considerate person
he had imagined. Rather she is a scheming seductress. In his
characteristic way of not understanding language, Philip fails
to "catch" the meaning of her pass until it is made explicit.

> ARAMINTA: Shall we go to bed?
> *(Brief silence.)*
> PHILIP: I'll . . . just go and get my coat.
> ARAMINTA: *(stares at him for a moment in blank incom-
> prehension, then realizes what he means. She
> stands up.)* I meant together. (Pp. 40–41)

Don, Philip's closest friend and counselor, seems until the
end of the play to be a sincerely dedicated teacher. His very
name suggests that he is a devoted English don who caringly
instructs his college students as well as confidants like Philip.

Yet he too turns out to be a fraud. In the last scene he confesses to Philip that he is a teacher devoted only to his own idleness, not to students, in whom he has no interest whatsoever. He performs his duties perfunctorily, doing precious little work but earning large amounts of money.

> DON: Oh, I live by a lie. In my case, the lie is that I am a teacher of English, when in fact I am paid a handsome sum by the college to perfect a technique of idleness which I hope will eventually become unparalleled in academic history. . . .
>
> And now, twenty four weeks a year, I simply select the relevant card and give my pupils the points they omitted in their essays, or if they've got them all I say, wonderful, see you next week, and I recover from this strenuous activity with twenty-eight weeks a year of total inactivity, usually in some pleasantly warm climate. (Pp. 74–75)

Liz, another of Philip's guests and the girl whom Don considers a suitable match for Philip, is, in a backward way, absolutely silent throughout the dinner party. She thus takes on the aura of a shy and innocent fawn. Later in the play we learn that she is in fact another sexually aggressive female. Assumed to be enamored of Philip, this deviously quiet girl has suddenly burst into a loud "overture" to Don, and he has willingly succumbed.

> DON: Well, Liz is . . . she's in my room now.
> PHILIP: Is she?
> DON: She's been there since yesterday evening. . . .
>
> PHILIP: I'm surprised, I didn't think you . . .
> DON: I'm surprised, too, in fact, I'm amazed. She's such a quiet girl, I mean, you don't expect her to be, I mean, it just sort of happened, and then for her

to be, well, so passionate, I was very surprised. (P. 77)

Celia, Philip's fiancée, at first gives the impression of being a loving and faithful girl friend. Several men, as she reports, have made sexual advances toward her, but she in her rectitude has accepted none of them. Hence, when she visits Philip's apartment on the morning following his party and discovers that Araminta has spent the night, she seems justified in scolding him. As she continues her tirade, however, she eventually unveils the truth about herself. She too has been unfaithful, for she has stayed the night in a hotel with Braham, another of Philip's guests. Furthermore, all the stories she told about her libidinous admirers were only lies, designed to make her appear sexually intriguing.

PHILIP: I'm not surprised you are having second thoughts, if all these people keep making passes at you all the time.

CELIA: What are you talking about?

PHILIP: Well, you know, Noakes and Johnson and all those people you were talking about last night.

CELIA: Oh, that.

PHILIP: Yes.

CELIA: None of that was true.

PHILIP: What?

CELIA: You know I'm always making things up.

PHILIP: Why?

CELIA: Well, you've got to say something, haven't you? Can't just sit there like a statue all evening. Like Liz. And lies are usually that much more interesting than the truth, that's all. (P. 62)

Admittedly, Celia's disloyalty is largely the result of Philip's own failure to understand her. At the end of his dinner party, when she hints to him that she wants to sleep with him and he again misses her meaning, her frustration leads her to seek consolation with someone else.

CELIA: Well, I did ask you to let me stay.
PHILIP: You didn't.
CELIA: Of course I did. I couldn't have made it much clearer if I'd started unbuttoning myself.
PHILIP: But I thought you just wanted to help with the washing up. (P. 52)

Yet Philip's blindness condones neither her infidelity nor her dishonest pose of innocence.

Braham, unlike the other dissemblers, never pretends to be morally superior. From the moment he enters the play until the moment he leaves, this amusingly irreverent yet unbearably cynical man does nothing but express his contempt for humanity and his refusal to do good deeds. Whether describing the telethon he hosted which, he nonchalantly announces, raised enough money to cover only his own fee, or discussing his general indifference to starving people, whom he views as worthless vermin,

BRAHAM: Nowadays, if I get one of those things through my letter box telling me I can feed an entire village for a week for the price of a prawn cocktail, I tear it up, throw it in my wastepaper basket, go out to my favorite restaurant and order a prawn cocktail. (P. 26)

he is constantly displaying his loathsome nature. He flaunts an unregenerate wickedness that is a foil to Philip's unstraying goodness.

While it is true that Braham always exposes his overall wickedness, this does not mean that he also exhibits his current evil intentions. In truth, he conceals them just as do all the other characters. At the end of the dinner party, when he offers to drive Celia home, he pretends that his gesture is nothing more than friendly. Later we realize, when we hear that he has spent the night with Celia, that he had planned to seduce her all the while.

> BRAHAM: (*Looks over to Celia.*) Can I give anyone a lift? Only one of you, I'm afraid, because it's only a two-seater. (P. 38)

Near the end of the play, while the characters' masks are still being removed and their true identities disclosed, Don himself summarizes the society in which he lives:

> You see, I always divide people into two groups. Those who live by what they know to be a lie, and those who live by what they believe, falsely, to be the truth. (P. 73)

In other words, everyone in his world is either a deliberate deceiver of others or an unconscious deceiver of himself. From the evidence that Hampton presents, Don's theory certainly seems to be valid. Each of the play's characters fits neatly into one of these two categories: Araminta, Don, Liz, Celia, and Braham, who are all actors playing parts, fall into the first group; Philip, who mistakenly believes that these people are exhibiting their true selves, is deluding himself and therefore fits into the second.

> DON: . . . Celia belonged to the first group and you [Philip] to the second. (P. 73)

However, in this illusory world, where so many asserted realities are also undermined, we question even Don's ostensibly accurate theory. It is a broad generalization and, like most others, cannot be accepted as fact.

> DON: What is wrong with the statement: "All generaliza-

tions are false"?
PHILIP: It's a generalization. (P. 74)

Indeed, under closer inspection Don's theory, with its strict either/or dividing line, disintegrates, for there is at least one person who fits into both categories and thereby negates it. Philip, it is true, is an unintentional self-deceiver, but he is also a deliberate deceiver of others.

Throughout act one Philip appears to be a philanthropist, a person who loves mankind unequivocally. Yet during act two it gradually becomes evident that he is actually a misanthrope in disguise, a disguise that he has consciously assumed. The disclosure of Philip's true identity, the ultimate and most startling unmasking of the play, takes place in two steps. The first occurs on the morning following his liaison with Araminta. She, his temptress, is the catalyst by which this revelation takes place. Ironically, instead of drawing forth the romantic side of his character, she brings to the surface only his misanthropic nature.

ARAMINTA: I always seem to bring out the worst in people.
(P. 46)

The night of heated sex that she had envisioned has turned out to be a fiasco. Philip was impotent. Araminta assumes that this misfortune was the result of a steadfast faithfulness to Celia that prevented him from being attracted to another.

ARAMINTA: I know, it's funny how important fidelity is to some people. I mean, it's something that never occurs to me. (P. 48)

Philip, however, offers her the correct explanation.

PHILIP: It wasn't that—the truth is, I don't really find you attractive. (P. 48)

For the first time in the play, Philip ceases to be his consistently
amicable self. He insults Araminta, acknowledging what he
considers to be her unappealing looks. We now realize that
Philip—even if unable to see past surfaces—does recognize
the most apparent shortcomings of people. He simply pretends
not to see them, for reasons at this point unknown to us. We
thus begin to suspect that a less than benevolent person lurks
beneath the façade of philanthropy.

The second step in his unveiling occurs during his confrontation with Celia after she has caught him with Araminta.
Philip tries to pacify his fiancée by telling her that he did not
actually have sex with his seductress and that he let her spend
the night only because he thought he would offend her if he
sent her away. Continuing his defense, he admits that his attempt to avoid insulting Araminta was motivated by an intense
fear that she would despise him if he did hurt her.

> PHILIP: I mean, I mean that the basic feature of my char-
> acter is an anxiety to please people and to do what
> they want, which leads to, that is, which amounts
> to a passion, and which is, in fact, so advanced that
> I can only describe it as . . . terror. (P. 68)

Most revealingly, he confesses that all his other "philanthropic"
pursuits, like this one, are stimulated not by a genuine love
of people, but by a desire to be loved himself.

> CELIA: Sympathy, is it, you're after?
> PHILIP: Well, yes, perhaps, yes, I suppose so. I don't know.
> Perhaps not sympathy. Liking.
> CELIA: At least you like everyone, that's half the battle,
> anyway.
> PHILIP: Yes, that's half the battle. The wrong half. (P. 65)

He wages a war of being kind to people only to win a far

more important battle, that of gaining everyone's favor. A victory of just the first would be meaningless to him, for success at liking everyone is not what he really seeks ("That's half the battle. The wrong half").

Even Philip's relationship with Celia is founded not so much on a profound affection for her as a desperate need to have someone love him—if not Celia, than almost any other halfway attractive woman who happens along. Terrified of being lonely, he ferrets out companionship wherever he can find it. Indeed, at the end of the play after Celia has deserted him, his reaction, following a brief depression, is simply to seek out Liz to fill the void that Celia has created.

> PHILIP: Well, when I was talking to Celia this afternoon, she asked me why I wanted to get married, I mean, apart from wanting to marry her. It made me realize that she was right, that I did want to get married, that I was lonely, now that youthful hopes have faded in the usual way, that it wasn't only her. It's all right when you're with people, when there's someone there, as long as there are people there to fill the air with plausible sounds. It's when the silence comes . . . you know, I find it whistles and rings now, the older I am, the louder it seems to get, the silence. I'm sorry, I didn't mean to get maudlin. . . .
> And I was thinking what you said to me yesterday about Liz. . . .
> Yes, you remember you were saying you thought she liked me, and that she would be more suitable for me than Celia. (Pp. 76–77)

Not only does Philip want to be liked, but also he will do anything to avoid the knowledge that he is disliked. The extreme and incredibly selfish measures to which he will resort to avoid such an awareness is revealed in a story that he tells to Celia: Several years ago, when he taught in Hong Kong, he used to meet a hunchback on the street who begged him for money. Everyday, wanting to appear charitable, Philip would give him some spare change. One day, however, he discovered that he had forgotten his money. Terrified that the hunchback would be angry with him, he jumped into his car, stamped his foot on the accelerator and sped out the car-park, accidentally hitting the beggar. Although he saw the crutches spring up in the air, he did not stop. Unable to face the prospect that someone might hate him, this acutely egoistic man raced desperately ahead, not even trying to help his seriously wounded victim.

Finally, in the same showdown between Celia and himself, Philip makes a statement that peels away the last layer of his disguise and removes any doubt of his misanthropic nature. Although he intends it to illustrate a point about man in general, this remark clearly reveals only Philip's individual feelings.

> PHILIP: You can like people without being an optimist. For instance, it's easier to like people if it occurs to you that they're going to die. It's difficult not to like a man if you can envisage his flesh falling from his bones. (Pp. 65–66)

Philip's enjoyment of the human race arises from a morbid pleasure he finds in imagining man dead. In this speech he does not say that he sympathizes with man for having to undergo postmortal processes. His gorily detailed description of physical decay shows that he takes comforting refuge in the thought of them. He literally likes man only on the condition that ("if") he can picture the flesh falling from his bones. Without this ugly vision as a shelter in which to hide from the unbearableness of life with other men, he would be unable to feign love of humanity. He would thus display himself as the misanthrope he really is.

With this statement, Celia herself realizes that Philip is not the totally benevolent person he has been portraying. Rather he is a man with a hidden but dominant sadistic side.

CELIA: I never realized you had a morbid streak in you. (P. 66)

She recognizes that she, herself a deceiver, has been reciprocally deceived, for Philip verges on being evil.

CELIA: My problem is, all the men I fall in love with turn out to be such terrible people. (P. 69)

We, who see beyond her individual situation to view that of the other characters in the play, also perceive that the entire swarm of pretenders who gather around and gull Philip have been duped by him in return.

Hampton's major purpose in writing his drama and putting us through this winding labyrinth of false appearances, in which everyone turns out to be both a deceiver and a deceived, is not immediately evident to us. When we first view *The Philanthropist* and discern its obvious kinship to Molière's *The Misanthrope,* it appears that his only intention is to have fun writing a modern-day, inside-out version of the seventeenth-century French comedy. Indeed, when we compare the two plays, we realize that Hampton has, in fact, written an extraordinarily tight paraphrase of *The Misanthrope* in which he maintains its broad structure and thematic conclusions but updates the action and inverts everything else. The plot outline and the central points of the earlier play are repeated in *The Philanthropist,* but the details of character and incident, within that outline, which lead us to those points, are reversed.[2]

---

2. Not only does Hampton parallel the content of *The Misanthrope,* but as an amusing inside joke, he also has his characters intermittently refer to Molière's comedy. At one point, for example, Braham tells the following story: Once when he went to the *Comédie Française* in Paris, a lady tourist asked him to explain the plot of the play they were watching. She had come too late to read the programme, and she did not understand what the actors were saying. His reply to her was: "Well, Madame, it's about a man who hates humanity so much that he would undoubtedly refuse to explain the plot of a world-famous play to an ignorant tourist" (p. 36). Clearly, the play they were observing was *The Misanthrope,* and Braham, the man who refused to explain its plot to the tourist, identified himself as a hater of humanity, similar to, but much more despicable than, the character in the play.

For instance, both plays include an incident, near or at the beginning, in which the title character and his best friend listen to and criticize the work of a creative writer. But whereas Philip, the philanthropist, praises John's amateurish play, Alceste, the misanthrope, lashes at Oronte's trite poetry; whereas, Don, the friend, cites predominantly the play's weaknesses, Philante, the comrade, points out mostly the poetry's merits; whereas John, the playwright, is infuriated with Philip for admiring his work, Oronte, the poet, is enraged at Alceste for scorning his. The conclusions that are drawn from these antithetical scenes, how-ever, are one and the same: extremist approaches in our dealing with people are dangerous for they tend to alienate us from those around us. Philip's excessive positivism repels John, for he considers such fulsome praise dishonest. Alceste's inordinate negativism turns away Oronte, because he finds such harsh criticism unfair. Hence in this scene, as in the rest of the play, it seems that Hampton's only purpose is to reexpress, from an opposite approach, the ideas of Molière.

In our minds, however, the firmly implanted image of John's fake suicide reminds us that we are to trust no appearances. If the thesis of *The Philanthropist* seems to be just a recapitula-tion of that of *The Misanthrope,* it probably is not. Hampton must have something additional on his mind, something that is less apparent. Indeed, as we scrutinize the play more carefully, we discover that Hampton does have a far greater purpose— to use his paraphrase of the earlier play to make his own per-sonal statement about the moral and intellectual condition that is fast approaching in England. Hampton has laid his play in the "near future" (p. 7) and thereby implies that it is intended as a warning about a state of existence soon to come.

In the opening "suicide" scene, Hampton reinforces our belief that this is his purpose through a play-within-a-play that specifically identifies the in-depth study of Philip as a disguised analysis of future day England. Following the completion of John's reading of his drama, he and his two critics make several comments which tell us that the play-within-a-play is a mirror reflection of the play itself. All the salient features of the one are prominant elements of the other.

John's drama has an opening scene that is Pirandello-like;

> DON: I can't really say I like that Pirandello-style beginning. (P. 11)

so has Hampton's. The first incident in *The Philanthropist,* John's reading of his drama, is typical of Pirandello in its use of a play-within-a-play to shed light on the play itself.

John's drama incorporates a heterogeneous mixture of theatrical ingredients;

> DON: . . . but you do try to give the customers a bit of everything—a touch of melodrama, the odd *coup de théâtre,* humour, tragedy, monologues, and pastoral interludes. (P. 10)

Hampton's includes all the same ones. Melodrama is represented by John's suicide, which we perceive as intensely dramatic before we know it is fake; "odd" *coup de théâtre* also by John's suicide, which we view as a bizarre and sensational turn of events once we realize it is fake; humor by the numerous witticisms made throughout; tragedy by the pain that Philip suffers upon being deserted by virtually everyone; monologues by long, continuous anecdotes such as Philip's one about the crippled beggar; pastoral interludes by certain musical passages, such as the rustic-toned "This Picture Is Enchantingly Beautiful" from Mozart's *The Magic Flute,* which are used as transitions between scenes.[3]

John's drama utilizes an ingenious technical device to make the suicide of a character appear authentic;

---

3. These musical passages—arias, symphonic movements, and a chorus—represent another sublevel on which the play is working, for their titles and the titles of the larger musical structures from which they emerge comment wittily on the action and characters of *The Philanthropist.* For example, "Where Friend's Tears Fall" from Mozart's *The Abduction from the Seraglio* is played at the conclusion of scene three, in which Philip, feeling remorse at what he is about to do, exits to the bedroom to join Araminta, his seductress.

JOHN: I think perhaps he might put the revolver in his
        mouth. Then, if the back wall of the set was white-
        washed, they could use some quaint device to cover
        it with great gobs of brain and bright blood at the
        vital moment. (P. 13)

Hampton's employs the identical one. When, in *The Philanthropist,* John accidentally shoots himself, demonstrating his
device with a gun that is unexpectedly loaded, Hampton represents this killing through the very device that John has just
described.

> *To illustrate, John puts the revolver into his mouth and
> presses the trigger. Loud explosion. By some quaint device,
> gobs of brain and bright blood appear on the whitewashed
> wall.* (P. 13)

John's drama assigns names to its characters that are symbolic
of what they represent;

JOHN: . . . in point of fact [Man] signifies man. (P. 10)

so does Hampton's. Philip is a philanthropist and philologist;
Don, a university don.

Finally and most notably, the presence of a single dramatic
character who represents the English people as a whole is found
not only in John's drama;

DON: I mean I don't know if this is right but I rather took
        [Man] to signify England. . . .

JOHN: . . . now you come to mention it, I suppose he could
        be taken to represent England.[4] (P. 10)

it is also contained in Hampton's. Philip is not a character
distinct from the others in his world. On the contrary, he is
a figure paradigmatic of the entire, future English society partly
depicted, partly described in the play, an embodiment of the

---

4. The passage from which these lines are taken actually begins by satirizing
critics who find meanings where they do not exist and who miss others that
obviously do. In midstream, however, it turns around and admits that subtle
and significant meanings often exist, sometimes where the author does not
intend them. In any case, Hampton confirmed to the writer in an interview in
London, on September 2, 1976, that he did intend Philip to represent England.

most serious weaknesses that Hampton believes are becoming increasingly prevalent in the British people. Indeed, as we look back at the play and reexamine the other characters in it as well as the people in the outside world, the discussion of whom forms a counterpoint to the main action, we realize that the two major weaknesses in Philip—the lack of moral fiber and the inability to see past surfaces—are also those of this whole, fast-approaching society.

Within the assortment of characters who actually appear in the play, there is no one who represents a center of moral consciousness. They are all dissolute individuals who conceal their nymphomania, idleness, infidelity, and generally evil intentions behind various disguises. The consensus among them is that the truth is insignificant

> DON: You know very well that unless you're a scientist, it's much more important for a theory to be shapely than for it to be true. (P. 20)

and also boring.

> CELIA: And lies are usually that much more interesting than the truth. (P. 62)

Consequently, honesty is avoided at all costs.[5]

---

5. Not only does Philip, on one level, represent England, but also, as Christopher Hampton divulged to the writer in the same interview on September 2, each of the play's seven immoral characters, on another level, embodies one of the Seven Deadly Sins. The writer guessed, correctly, according to Hampton, that: Philip, who gorges himself with chocolates (p. 10), and cereal (p. 49), and other foods throughout the play, is Gluttony; Don, the indolent professor who does a mimimal amount of work, is Sloth; Braham, whose love of money is the primary motivation for writing books, hosting telethons, and even leaving his wife (he parts with her for tax reasons!) is Avarice; John, who seethes with anger when Philip praises his play, is Wrath; Araminta, who has an insatiable desire for men, is Lust; Liz, who conceals her love of Don, and also Philip, because she believes it would be unladylike to express it openly, is Pride.

DON: I'm sure she'd marry you like a shot if you asked her.
PHILIP: Do you think so?
DON: I'm sure of it.
PHILIP: She hasn't said anything to me about it.
DON: Well, she has her pride. (P. 20)

Hampton has added to the writer's guesses that Celia, a generally ambitious girl who creates lies about male suitors to appear as desirable as other women she admires, is Envy.

Similarly, from what we hear about the people in the anarchistic world outside, they too lack a moral backbone. Among them the prominent figures are a hedonistic Queen of England, who is concerned only with her personal pleasures and not with affairs of state (when she hears about grave events in Parliament, she ignores them and instead sends for the Minister of Sport to restring her trampoline), licentious priests who seduce young boys on trains, and most of all, numerous lunatics terrorizing England with their violent assassinations of British politicians and writers.

In one particular incident of multiple murder that is reported, a jovial English lady bicycles to Parliament, enters the gallery to watch a session of government, takes out a sub-machine gun, and "mows down" the Prime Minister and several other politicians. She subsequently removes the costume she is wearing and reveals that she is actually a he—a lieutenant who illogically believes that he is saving England from creeping socialism by killing members of a Tory government. Significantly, we see in the incident of the disguised radical—described by Braham with the histrionic term *comic figure*—that the playing of roles to mask evil intentions is not a phenomenon circumscribed within the world of the play.

> BRAHAM: . . . you must admit the way this man went about
> it did show a kind of rudimentary dramatic flair.
> (P. 25)

It exists and is probably rampant in the world outside.

The second major weakness in Philip, the inability to see past surfaces, is also a serious limitation of this whole British society. In the case of the characters who appear in the play, this weakness takes the form of a general inability to see beyond the outer brightness of matters to view the inner darkness—an inability to give serious attention to problems that have their comic aspect but are essentially tragic. It is this shortcoming that puts them in the precarious position of being overwhelmed

by the encroaching violence.

Early in the play, in an incident that exposes reflexes typical of the play's characters, Don reacts to John's accidental self-annihilation by laughing at blackly humorous puns concerning it.

> PHILIP: Celia wasn't very sympathetic either. The first thing she said when I rang her up and told her about it was: "I'm not surprised, [John's] always been ludicrously absent-minded. . . ."
>
> DON: (*He laughs, recovers, shakes his head.*) No, it was a terrible thing to happen, really. (*He tries to look solemn, but is suddenly overcome by helpless laughter.*) (P. 15)

Although he tries to be somber, this desensitized character finds it difficult to take seriously even a grotesque death that he himself has witnessed.

Later, during the dinner party and other sequences of the play, the rest of the characters, especially Braham, respond to tragic occurrences in a similar manner. As they sit around and discuss current events, they amuse themselves by describing the absurdity of the violent acts that are taking place throughout England—acts that admittedly are amusing, if only in a macabre way. Yet they fail to recognize the tragedy that is also inherent in these happenings. Shut off in their university world, discussing these events at a distance, they believe that what is taking place outside cannot possibly affect them.

> PHILIP: But . . . what's going to happen?
>
> DON: Oh, I don't know, coalition government, another election, something like that. It's not going to make much difference, whatever happens.
>
> PHILIP: Isn't it?
>
> DON: Not to us, anyway. (P. 18)

Although they themselves are actually being threatened by this creeping violence—a violence that is already starting to filter through into their own homes, as is symbolized by John's shocking self-slaughter in Philip's apartment—they cannot see that they are in danger.

The extremity of that blindness is displayed in Braham's reaction to an assassination plot against several top British writers. When he hears that F.A.T.A.L. (the Fellowship of Allied Artists Against Literature) has made a list of twenty-five of the most respected English writers, all of whom it intends to kill, he is insulted that he, himself a popular novelist, is not on the list. Unable to grasp that there is a real and immediate threat facing these writers (two have already been brutally murdered), he is outraged only at the "assassination" of his own ego.

Hampton briefly suggests, through the voice of Braham, that the people in the outside world also fail to comprehend the tragedy of what is happening in England. Braham makes known, in his usual insouciant manner, that the rest of this society shares the same amused and aloof attitude toward the nation's crumbling condition as do the characters in the play.[6]

> BRAHAM: I must say, the great thing about all this is it shows we're [the English people] accepting our decadence with a certain stylishness. (P. 25)

There is in the outside world, however, another form of inability to see past surfaces that is of more personal concern to Hampton as writer. Like Philip, many of the other people

---

6. Describing *Savages'* protagonist, Alan West, in an interview prior to the opening of that play, Hampton indirectly reflects on the basic indifference of the Western society depicted in *The Philanthropist* to crucial political and social problems: "The only way he is really involved is through his overriding interest in Brazilian Indian legends. He has a classic Western liberal approach to the situation. It's only when it comes to his doorstep that he thinks in a way which is not distanced and dissociated. I think that's true of people in England. If there's one thing the English public is less interested in than the theatre, it's politics" (W. Stephen Gilbert, "Hampton's Court," *Plays and Players,* ed. Peter Ansorge [London, 1973], p. 36).

in this society are too shortsighted or literal-minded to discern important meanings in literature. They cannot dig beneath the words, the style, or the particularities of plot and character to unearth the grain of truth that is relevant in the actual world.

The members of F.A.T.A.L., who are murdering popular British writers, are doing so because these assassins believe that all literature presents a false picture of life. They do not understand that fiction often parallels the real world.

> CELIA [*reading a letter from F.A.T.A.L.*]: It is our belief that no human being who devotes his life and energy to the manufacture of fantasies can be anything but fundamentally inadequate. (P. 59)

Similarly, James Boot, a university student, whose story is told in detail by Don, also regards literature as a worthless heap of untruths. Boot, who had recently been studying political and economic works and who had subsequently fallen into a deep state of despair over the problems of Western democracy, at one point locked himself in a room for several days and tried to solve these problems. Ultimately, when he failed, he piled all his books in the middle of his room and burned them as testimony to the hopelessness of Western democracy. During the period of his depression, Don visited him and suggested that he forget these problems and return to his study of Wordsworth. Boot's reply to him, according to Don, was:

> "[Wordsworth] had nothing to do with anything, and his work, like all art, was a lot of self-indulgent shit which had no relevance to our problems and was no help at all to man or beast." (P. 30)

He is incapable of recognizing that Wordsworth's view of existence, though romanticized, presents universal truths pertinent even in the mundane world, perhaps even to his own problems.

In the final scene of the play, Hampton has Philip perform

an action and deliver a speech that leave the audience with an afterthought. Philip, whose private world is crumbling around him and who is despondent, takes a pistol from his desk as if to commit suicide. Before pulling the trigger, however, he telephones Don, tells him that he is about to do something terrible, but first recites his latest anagram.

> PHILIP: "imagine the theatre as real" . . . it's an anagram for "I hate thee sterile anagram." (P. 78)

After hanging up the phone, he takes the pistol . . . points it toward himself . . . pulls the trigger . . . and ignites a fire.

Philip's pistol is not a pistol at all. Rather it is a cigarette lighter. As in the opening visual metaphor, Hampton hoodwinks us, his intention being to signal us that we are to trust no appearances. This time, as is suggested by the association of the deceptive action with the content of Philip's anagram, he wants us to realize that although the world on stage is fictional, and seems to be remote from that in which we live, it is in fact a close approximation of the actual world. Early in *The Philanthropist* Hampton established that for Philip and Don, the audience watching John's play, there were striking similarities between what happened on stage and what happened off: notably, just as a character in John's play fatally shot himself, so too John, going through the motions of the suicide scene for the second time, dies by his own gunshot. Now, in the final scene of *The Philanthropist,* Hampton indirectly tells his own audience, through Philip's anagram, that it too should recognize "the theatre as real."

Philip, who has made no emotional or intellectual progress during the play, would have to fantasize, for he does not really believe, that drama offers a perspective of the actual world ("imagine the theatre as real"). Still literal-minded, he remains incapable of seeing beneath literature's outer skin of fiction to discern and be enlightened by the important truths reflected in its deeper, fertile regions. Sadly, he continues to immerse himself in word games that even he begins to detest for their purposelessness and inability to nourish ("I hate thee sterile anagram").

It is hoped that we, upon viewing *The Philanthropist,* will not be so shortsighted as the professor who could not even recognize Man as an allegorical figure for everyman. Presented with Hampton's deliberate test of "multileveledness," we will uncover one by one the various layers of meaning, and perhaps benefit from the gathered awareness we achieve by the time we reach its heart.

3 *"A Vicious Triangle"*: Old Times *by Harold Pinter*

Dorothy Tutin, Vivien Merchant (intentionally almost invisible), and Colin Blakely in the opening scene of *Old Times*, original London production directed by Peter Hall, 1971. *Photograph courtesy of Donald Cooper.*

A s the curtain rises on the first scene of Harold Pinter's *Old Times,* all three of the play's characters are on-stage, placed at separate positions so that their figures form a triangle. Deeley and his wife, Kate, in whose converted farmhouse the play takes place, are seated at two points upstage and in the light. They are awaiting the arrival of Kate's old friend Anna, whom Kate has not seen for twenty years. At the same time, Anna, the expected guest, is standing behind them, at a position in the back of the stage and in the dark. Paradoxically, her figure is present although she has not yet arrived.

In this opening tableau, Pinter presents a visual metaphor that evokes the two central themes of the play. The paradoxical presence of Anna and the triangle made up of all three characters form a symbolic picture which introduces us to the ideas that are explored throughout.

The first of these themes, which is suggested by Anna's enigmatic occupation of the room, is that the past exists in the present through memory, and that it therefore has potential impact on the present. Indeed, if we analyze the visual image of Anna in relation to the opening dialogue between Deeley and Kate, we recognize that Anna's figure, at the beginning of the play, represents the past which has been captured in Kate's mind through memory and which has the power to affect her current life.

As the action begins, Deeley is questioning his wife about

the old times the two women shared twenty years ago. From the answers that Kate gives, it soon becomes evident that she recalls virtually nothing about that past. As she indicates by the isolated, first word of the play, *dark,* she sees only a blank as she looks back at those times long gone. Although Anna was once her one and only friend, with whom she spent much of her youth, Kate insists: "I hardly remember her. I've almost totally forgotten her."[1] Kate, apparently, has repressed memories of some frightening (a second meaning of *dark*[2]) past shared with Anna that poses a threat to the present.

Thus we see that Kate's memories, which have been hidden in the dark spaces at the back of her mind, are embodied in Anna's figure, which, similarly, is obscured in the shadowy area at the back of the stage. Just as these memories loom over Kate and Deeley as a menace to the present, so too Anna's portentous figure lurks behind them as some form of threat. Later in the play the drawing of those memories back into the light of consciousness is represented by the movement of Anna into the light at the front of the stage. It is at this point that Anna, the dramatic character, arrives at the farmhouse (a transition accomplished without any explicit "arrival" or time gap) and begins to unleash her own frightening memories, inciting Kate to illuminate her own.

ANNA

Queuing all night, the rain, *do you remember?* my goodness, the Albert Hall, Covent Gardens, *what did we eat?* to look

---

1. Harold Pinter, *Old Times* (New York: Grove Press, Inc., 1971), p. 12. Page references in the text are all to this edition.
2. The third and perhaps most apparent meaning of *dark,* suggested by its context of physical description, is that Anna was of an olive complexion.

KATE

(*Reflectively.*) Dark.
Pause

DEELEY

Fat or thin?

KATE

Fuller than me. I think.   (P. 7)

back, half the night, to do things we loved, we were young then of course, but what stamina, and to work in the morning, and to a concert, or the opera, or the ballet, that night, *you haven't forgotten?* and then riding on top of the bus down Kensington High Street, and the bus conductors, and then dashing for the matches for the gasfire and then I suppose scrambled eggs, *or did we? who cooked?* both giggling and chattering, both huddling to the heat, then bed and sleeping, and all the hustle and bustle in the morning, rushing for the bus again for work, lunchtimes in Green Park, exchanging all our news, with our very own sandwiches, innocent girls, innocent secretaries, and then the night to come and goodness knows what excitement in store, I mean the sheer expectation of it all, the looking-forwardness of it all, and so poor, but to be poor and young, and a girl, in London then . . . and the cafés we found, almost private ones, *weren't they?* where artists and writers and sometimes actors collected, and others with dancers, we sat hardly breathing with our coffee, heads bent, so as not to be seen, so as not to disturb, so as not to distract, and listened and listened to all those words, all those cafés and all those people, creative undoubtedly, *and does it still exist I wonder? do you know? can you tell me?* (Pp. 17–18; emphasis added)

It is with this provoking of Kate to recall her memories that the threat of the past begins its course toward full realization.

Once Anna, Kate, and also Deeley (who, as we discover, knew Kate and Anna when they lived together) start to delve into the past, they do so by relating elaborate anecdotes about it. In the course of hearing these stories, we soon detect, through obvious parallels, that all three characters are reminiscing about the same incidents. We also recognize, however, that there are notable discrepancies and contradictions between various accounts. Each character describes these incidents from his own viewpoint, unconsciously distorting the past to satisfy his own needs. Indeed, an important idea that is related to the play's first major theme is that one can never be certain that the past existed as one remembers it, for the past is gone and only the memories of it remain. Furthermore, one's memories are not necessarily accurate recordings of the past, for they often redefine it, either distorting it to hide what is threatening or creating a totally fictitious past to fulfill one's current psychological needs.

ANNA
There are some things one remembers even though they may never have happened. There are things I remember which may never have happened but as I recall them so they take place. (Pp. 31–32)

Therefore, because the characters themselves are never sure of what took place in their past, we, the audience, who know only as much as they tell us, are necessarily left in a similar state of uncertainty. Nevertheless, we still try to synthesize the information we are given to establish certain realities about that past.

Of the many stories that these characters relate, there are two told by Deeley and Anna which are pivotal in allowing the threat of the past to be actualized. Together, these two stories expose the focus of menace that has caused Kate to repress all her memories of Anna. The information that we gather from them suggests that a lesbian relationship may once have existed between the two women.

At one point Deeley recounts the following story, disclosing the way in which he first met Kate: One Sunday afternoon he went to a cinema to see the Robert Newton film *Odd Man Out*. Before the movie began, he noticed that there were only two people in the theater—two lesbian usherettes standing in the foyer, one sensuously stroking her breasts to seduce the other. At the end of the film he again saw only two people. One was the first usherette, who was exhausted, apparently having had sex with the second. The other, however, was Kate, the only other customer in the theater, to whom Deeley introduced himself. The second usherette was no longer present.

Having paid little attention to Deeley's story, Anna later tells a brief one of her own: One Sunday she and Kate slipped off to some obscure movie theater where "almost alone, [they] saw a wonderful film called Odd Man Out" (p. 38).

The parallels between these two stories (Deeley and Anna both saw *Odd Man Out,* on a Sunday, in a theater that was nearly empty, at the same time as Kate) suggest that Deeley and Anna are describing the same incident. We therefore assume that all three characters were together in the same theater, at the same time. There is, however, one major contradiction between the two stories for which we must account. Deeley claims that Kate was the only other customer in the theater, while Anna indicates that she was there as well. The most obvious explanation for this contradiction is that Anna was, in fact, in the theater but that Deeley mistook her for an usherette. In addition, Kate may have been the other female whom he identified as an usherette. This would explain why at the end of the film he saw only one usherette: he never assumed that Kate was the missing one. Furthermore, Anna implies through a sexual pun on the word *come* (she plays off of Deeley's own bawdy use of the word: "He went twice and came once" [p. 33]) that she and Kate had gone to the cinema for a sexual encounter, and thus may have been the lesbians whom Deeley saw.

ANNA
I remember one Sunday she said to me, looking up from the paper, come quick, quick, come with me quickly, and we seized our handbags and went, on a bus, to some totally obscure, some totally unfamiliar district, and, almost alone, saw a wonderful film called Odd Man Out. (P. 38)

The intimations of a lesbian relationship hardly stop here.

Throughout the play Anna constantly hints at it, without ever explicitly acknowledging its having existed.

> ANNA
> Ah, those songs. We used to play them, all of them, all the time, late at night, lying on the floor, lovely old things. Sometimes I'd look at her face, but she was quite unaware of my gaze. (P. 26)

Deeley, who is acutely sensitive to her innuendos, becomes so tormented by her deliberate failure to confess or deny that she and Kate were lovers that he tries repeatedly to draw conclusive information from her. When, for example, Anna hints at a homosexual attachment by using words such as *lest* and *gaze,* suggesting *lesbian* and *gay,* Deeley asks her to explain why she has chosen those particular words, the use of which seems awkward.

> ANNA
> No one who lived here would want to go far. I would not want to go far, I would be afraid of going far, lest when I returned the house would be gone
> DEELEY
> Lest?
> ANNA
> What?
> DEELEY
> The word lest. Haven't heard it for a long time. (P. 19)

> ANNA
> Sometimes I'd look at her face, but she was quite unaware of my gaze.
> DEELEY
> Gaze?
> ANNA
> What?

DEELEY
The word gaze. Don't hear it very often. (P. 26)

Unfortunately for Deeley, his suspense is never ended. Neither he nor the audience ever learns for certain whether or not the two women were lovers. In spite of all the hints that Anna drops, pointing to such a liaison, she never says anything definitive. Consequently, both Deeley and the audience are left to ponder this relationship, which ultimately remains ambiguous to us all.

Whether or not Anna and Kate ever engaged in a physical relationship, however, there is no question that Anna did possess amorous feelings toward Kate, even if Kate did not necessarily have reciprocal ones. Moreover, judging from the strange behavior that Anna evinces upon her arrival at the farmhouse, we recognize that she is still strongly attracted to Kate.

Most importantly, we also recognize that Anna's purpose in coming to visit the married couple is to win Kate as her lover. She intends to do so by conjuring up memories of the past, reestablishing her old intimacy with Kate, and ultimately drawing out of Kate any sexual feelings she may still possess for Anna. As Anna slyly insinuates in the following passage, she is going to probe beneath the surfaces of the present to look for passions from the past that she believes remain in the depths of Kate's being:

And I knew that Katey would always wait not just for the first emergence of ripple but for the ripples to pervade and pervade the surface, for of course as you know ripples on the surface indicate a shimmering in depth down through every particle of water down to the river bed. (Pp. 36–37)

She hopes that when those passions are elicited and set loose, they will motivate Kate to leave Deeley and become her lover.

As a result, Anna will usurp Deeley's position as Kate's sexual partner, while he will replace Anna as the "odd man out."

The second major theme introduced in the opening visual metaphor—a theme embodied in the triangle formed by the three characters—is that these people are involved in a love triangle in which, at any single time, two of the parties are joined in a tight sexual bond while the third is the "odd man out." As it happens, two of the three parties in this *ménage à trois,* Deeley and Anna, fight for the love of the third, Kate. Whenever one is winning, the other becomes the outsider unable for the moment to maintain a hold on Kate's love.

At the beginning of the play, the opening visual metaphor reveals that Deeley and Kate are the united pair, while Anna is the "odd man out." Kate and Deeley, happily tied in marriage, are symbolically linked by the similar positions they share in the light at the front of the stage. Anna, on the other hand, is in the shadows at the back of the stage, out of touch with the married couple. Kate has separated Anna from Deeley and herself by successfully burying her memories of Anna.

As soon as Anna arrives at the farmhouse, however, she once again asserts herself as a competitor for Kate. Sensing this, Deeley puts himself on guard against her advances, wittily but desperately struggling to defend his position as Kate's lover. The result is a quietly explosive battle between Anna and Deeley, in which each, maintaining icy coolness, uses a variety of tactics to win Kate's affection.

Of these tactics, there are three in particular, two used by Deeley, the other by Anna, that set off the muted fireworks. The first, which is employed by Deeley, is to hint that his possession of Kate is so firm that Anna should give up trying to win her. He first does this when, in describing his initial meeting with Kate, at *Odd Man Out,* he warns Anna that it was the leading man, Robert Newton, "who brought us together and it is only Robert Newton who can tear us apart" (p. 30), insinuating that Anna cannot destroy his secure marriage. Ironically, what Deeley does not realize is that, according to

Anna, it was she who brought Kate to the theater where Deeley met her. Therefore, by his logic it is she who can tear them apart.

Later in the play Deeley again uses this strategy in a musical tug-of-war for Kate's love. In this musical competition, both he and Anna try to establish a grip on Kate, but they do this in different ways. Anna attempts to seduce Kate by expressing passion for her. Deeley tries to defeat Anna's purpose by showing her once again that Kate is strongly bound to him in marriage. To achieve their goals, both characters take perfectly innocent lyrics from popular songs of the past and infuse them with erotic overtones.

ANNA

(*Singing.*) The way you comb your hair . . .
[Anna admits to Kate that she is sexually attracted to her.]
DEELEY

(*Singing.*) Oh no they can't take that away from me . . .
[Deeley warns Anna that she cannot steal Kate from him.]
ANNA

(*Singing.*) Oh but you're lovely, with your smile so warm . . .
[Anna persists in expressing her love for Kate and her beauty.]

DEELEY

(*Singing.*) I've got a woman crazy for me. She's funny that way.
Slight pause
[Deeley insists first that Kate is mad for him, not Anna, and secondly that Kate is unalterably set in her heterosexual or "that way" mode of life.]
ANNA

(*Singing.*) You are the promised kiss of springtime . . .
[Anna tells Kate that she longs to realize their relationship which, though once promised, was never fulfilled.]
DEELEY

(*Singing.*) And someday I'll know that moment divine, When all the things you are, are mine!
Slight pause

[Deeley asserts that he, eventually, will be the victor in the
battle for Kate; in so being, he will gain total possession
of her and "all the things" she is.]

ANNA

(*Singing*.) I get no kick from champagne,
Mere alcohol doesn't thrill me at all,
So tell me why should it be true—

DEELEY

(*Singing*.) That I get a kick out of you?
Pause
[Anna starts to tell Kate that she is the only stimulant which
can excite her sexual appetite; but before she can finish,
Deeley interrupts and snatches the lines from her, indicating
that he intends to seize Kate in the same fashion. He, alone,
will ever "get a kick out of" her.]

ANNA

(*Singing*.) They asked me how I knew
My true love was true,
I of course replied,
Something here inside
Cannot be denied.

[Anna confesses that her homosexual feelings for Kate are
too powerful to remain hidden.]

DEELEY

(*Singing*.) When a lovely flame dies . . .
[Deeley implies that whatever feelings Kate may have had
for Anna in the past, they are dead now.]

ANNA

(*Singing*.) Smoke gets in your eyes.
[Anna argues that Deeley's vision of the whole situation
is clouded. The "lovely flame" has not died; it still burns
brightly.] (Pp. 27–28)

Anna employs the second major device, which is to help
Kate rediscover her old feelings for Anna by compelling her
to journey through space—space in this play being a metaphor

for time. To understand how this subtle device works, we must first understand how Pinter uses the metaphor of time and space throughout the play.

In the opening visual image, Pinter first establishes the metaphor. The spatial relationship set up between Anna and the married couple represents the temporal one that also exists between them. Just as Anna's figure occupies the area in back of Deeley and Kate, so too the period that she represents, the two women's past as captured in Kate's memory, lies behind the present in which they live. In addition, if we view Anna as a dramatic character and not just as the embodiment of Kate's hidden memories, then we recognize that her looking out of a window, peering off into space, represents her own viewing of the distant past.

Later in the play Pinter continues the metaphor by having his characters refer to time in terms of space.

DEELEY

I have my eye on a number of pulses, pulses all round the globe, deprivations and insults, why should I waste valuable *space* listening to two—(P. 67; emphasis added)

Most importantly, Pinter symbolizes the temporal sphere in which Kate has remained by the spatial one in which she has also rested. Early in the play he establishes that she has not only confined herself to the present; she has also stayed essentially fixed in her remote farmhouse outside of London.

DEELEY
We rarely get to London. (P. 18)

DEELEY
My work takes me away quite often, of course. But Kate stays here (P. 19)

Just as Kate has avoided delving into the past, she has similarly refrained from journeying into the outside world. She senses that if she were to go into that realm, she would overstep the safe limits of the present and in this way jeopardize her relationship with Deeley.

Anna also is aware that movement through space represents movement through time. Furthermore, because she recognizes that traveling into the past would prove perilous to Kate's marriage, she too knows that Kate has been wise not to stray far from home.

> ANNA
>
> No one who lived here would want to go far. I would not want to go far, I would be afraid of going far, lest when I returned the house [symbolic of Kate and Deeley's firmly established marriage] would be gone. (P. 19)

Anna understands that by remaining in a closed corner of space, Kate metaphorically has stayed in the present and kept silent about the past.

> ANNA
>
> How wise you were to choose this part of the world, and how sensible and courageous of you both to stay permanently in such a silence. (P. 19)

However, because Anna's goal is to shatter that marriage and reconstruct her own relationship with Kate, she intends to persuade Kate to travel to other spaces and thereby journey into the past. Anna hopes that Kate, by doing so, will rediscover her old passion for Anna, leave Deeley, and reunite herself with Anna.

Put into practice, Anna's strategy proves to be a success. As we see, when Kate does start to delve (in thought if not in deed) into the outside world, she pairs herself with Anna and Deeley becomes separated from her. Near the end of act one Anna manages to spark in Kate an interest in Sicily, the far-away island on which she lives and also a spot that represents the distant past shared by both women.[3] She entices her mind to wander beyond what Pinter depicts as the quiet and peaceful shores of the present:

> ANNA
> Listen. What silence. Is it always as silent?
> DEELEY
> It's quite silent here, yes. Normally.
> *Pause*
> You can hear the sea sometimes if you listen very carefully. (P. 19)

> ANNA
> And the sky is so still.
> *Pause*
> Can you see that tiny ribbon of light? Is that the sea? Is that the horizon? (P. 22)

to reach the tumultuous landscape of the past that threatens to erupt and engulf the marriage.

> DEELEY
> You live on a very different coast.
> ANNA
> Oh, very different. I live on a volcanic island. (P. 22)

Kate's dangerous immersion in Sicily is realized in a sudden outpouring of questions about that exotic island and Anna's

---

3. Pinter's vision of time as a spatial terrain and the past as a distant area of land on it—that is, Kate and Anna's past equals Sicily—is most explicitly expressed in the key, opening line from *The Go-Between*:

> COLSTON'S VOICE
> The past is a foreign country. They do things differently there.

(Harold Pinter, *The Go-Between*, in *Five Screenplays* [New York: Grove Press, 1973], p. 287.) This screenplay, written by Pinter in 1970 during the same period as *Old Times*, shares its central theme—the effect of the past, through memory, on the present.

home on it. It is precisely at the point when Kate asks these questions that the conversation, which had previously taken place among all three characters, suddenly becomes only two-way. Deeley is excluded. No matter how hard he tries to interpose himself in the conversation, the two women refuse to listen to what he says.

KATE

(*To* ANNA.) Do you have marble floors?

ANNA

Yes.

KATE

Do you walk in bare feet on them?

ANNA

Yes. But I wear sandals on the terrace, because it can be rather severe on the soles.

KATE

The sun, you mean? The heat?

ANNA

Yes.

DEELEY

I had a great crew in Sicily. A marvellous cameraman. Irving Shultz. Best in the business. We took a pretty austere look at the women in black. The little old women in black. I wrote the film and directed it. My name is Orson Welles.

KATE

(*To* ANNA.) Do you drink orange juice on your terrace in the morning, and bullshots at sunset, and look down at the sea?

ANNA

Sometimes, yes.

DEELEY

As a matter of fact I am at the top of my profession, as a matter of fact, and I have indeed been associated with substantial numbers of articulate and sensitive people, mainly prostitutes of all kinds.

KATE

(*To* ANNA.) And do you like the Sicilian people? (Pp. 41–42)

Deeley warns Kate to forget about Sicily, for he too knows that her interest in it represents a renewed concern for the past—a concern that he himself fears is forcing him into the position of "odd man out" and, in the process, destroying his marriage.

DEELEY

I've been there. There's nothing more to see, there's nothing more to investigate, nothing. There's nothing more in Sicily to investigate. (P. 43)

His admonition, however, proves futile, for Kate persists in asking Anna: "Do you like the Sicilian people?" (P. 43). Consequently, the conversation continues to be a dialogue, and it remains such for the rest of act one. Anna, at least temporarily, has succeeded in reestablishing a tight bond between Kate and herself, thus separating Deeley from his wife.

Yet Deeley does not accept being the outsider for long. At the beginning of act two, while Kate is taking a bath, he employs one final strategy in a desperate effort to recapture his hold on Kate. It is at this point that the last movement of the play begins.

Deeley is aware that Anna's ultimate success or failure at permanently winning Kate will depend on whether or not she can prove that the lesbian relationship (whether physical or just emotional) she hints at was indeed a reality. If she can, then she might also be able to remind Kate of actual feelings she had for her that will compel Kate to leave Deeley and come live with her. Deeley also realizes that memories are the one tool that Anna has for verifying such a relationship. Therefore, in his endeavor to defeat her purpose, he tries to under-

mine the truthfulness of those memories and thereby destroy
her major weapon in the battle for Kate.

Deeley's means of invalidating her memories is to prove
that memories in general cannot be trusted. He shows that
one can recall any number of events that never really happened. Therefore, one can hardly rely on memories to know
what actually occurred in the past. Anna suggested earlier in
the play that one often remembers events that "may never have
happened." Now Deeley reiterates this idea for his own purposes.

During the conversation that Deeley and Anna have while
Kate is taking her bath, Deeley makes a statement about the
arrangement of beds (the second act takes place in the bedroom) that has two major implications.

DEELEY

We sleep here. These are beds. The great thing about these
beds is that they are susceptible to any amount of permutation. They can be separated as they are now. Or placed at
right angles, or one can bisect the other, or you can sleep
feet to feet, or head to head, or side by side. It's the castors
that make all this possible. (P. 48)

The first implication is that just as there are many possible
ways of rearranging the beds, so too there is an infinite number of ways of reconstructing the past. Not only can one re-
orient the beds to form several different patterns, but also
one can restring events together to create endless variations
of what happened long ago. Although the separate events
themselves may be based on fact, the product of relinking them
is likely to be fictitious.

The second implication is that he is about to invent a variation which suggests that he and Anna were lovers. Clearly,
his mention of the beds as being "susceptible to any amount
of permutation" insinuates that all possible pairings in this love
triangle have at some point taken place. Secondly, his use of the
word *bisect*, echoing *bisexual* (he now takes part in the game

of sexual innuendo that Anna began earlier), hints that Anna did indeed love men like himself, not just women.

Directly following this speech, Deeley unfolds his variation, a story about a London pub called the Wayfarer's Tavern, where he claims he used to see Anna (as well as another woman, whom we assume was Kate). His sole purpose in fabricating this story is to demonstrate to Anna that memories are often false and therefore cannot be taken seriously. As he begins, he hints, rather absurdly, that Anna was once a tart who may have had sexual relations with the men who frequented the tavern. When he specifically states that she was the "darling of the saloon bar" who was "looked after" by escorts who bought her drinks, he intimates that these men were paying for more than just cocktails (pp. 49–50). Later, when he says that he himself bought her drinks and that when he "gazed" (again playing Anna's game, this time mocking her earlier use of this word) up her skirt she found his gaze "perfectly acceptable," he suggests that she may have agreed to have sex with him (p. 51).

Unhappily for Deeley, for two reasons this last strategy fails to work. The first is that Anna, detecting the scheme behind his story, devises a counterscheme to defeat it. Throughout his story, before and after she realizes his intentions, Anna insists that none of the events he is describing ever took place.

ANNA

I don't think so.

I don't honestly think so.

I've rarely heard a sadder story. (Pp. 48–52)

Yet when his mocking use of the word *gaze* signals to her that he has invented the whole story to undermine hers,

DEELEY
You didn't object, you found my gaze perfectly acceptable.

ANNA
I was aware of your gaze, was I, (P. 51)

she decides that she will later admit that his story is true
and in this way show that all memories, including her own,
can be accepted as fact. She waits until much later, when her
confession will have full shock effect, and then triumphantly
concedes that he did indeed "gaze" up her skirt.

ANNA
I had borrowed some of her underwear, to go to a party.
Later that night I confessed. It was naughty of me. She
stared at me, nonplused, perhaps, is the word. But I told
her that in fact I had been punished for my sin, for a man
at the party had spent the whole evening looking up my
skirt (P. 65)

The second reason that Deeley's strategy fails to work is that
by this time, Anna's exposing of memories and prompting of
Kate to journey through time and space have already resulted
in a lasting transformation of Kate's sexual preference. Kate
has permanently shifted her love from Deeley to Anna, and
consequently, nothing he does can prevent him from being
the outsider.

The bath, which Kate entered at the end of act one and
which she completes following his story, symbolizes the total
rejection of Deeley and acceptance of Anna. That Kate has
already begun to bathe before the story indicates that the turnabout of her love has by now been irreversibly set in motion.
The significance of this bath is drawn from a story that Kate
tells concerning another bath that she took, during the time
that she lived with Anna: One night Anna had been lying in
bed, sleeping, when Kate entered her room and began to stare
down at her. Perceiving Anna as being dead and having dirt

all over her face, Kate decided to take a bath and cleanse herself thoroughly. Once she had finished, she returned to the room, brought Deeley in from outside, and then discovered that Anna was gone. Subsequently, when Deeley made sexual advances to her, she at first rejected them, throwing the dirt from a flower pot into his face. Afterwards, when he suggested that she marry him and that they both go live in a new environment, she consented.

The significance of the bath is that it symbolizes a stripping and cleansing by which Kate divests herself of one environment and surrounds herself with another. It represents her renouncement of a mysterious existence with Anna—an existence that, as suggested by her impression of Anna's reclining figure, she viewed as dirty and that she would now consider dead and buried—in favor of a heterosexual one as Deeley's wife. Although she temporarily rejects Deeley's sexual advances, believing that all sex is filthy (as is suggested by her throwing dirt on him), she eventually agrees to be his wife.

When Kate takes the bath, at the end of act one, one senses that again she is stripping herself of one life style and enveloping herself in another. This time, however, she is reverting to her former way of life with Anna. The reversal in the arrangement of furniture seen on stage at the beginning of act two, directly following Kate's entering the bath, underscores the idea that her act washing marks a turnabout of her affection.

The divans and armchair are disposed in precisely the same relation to each other as the furniture in the first act, but in reversed positions. (P. 47)

Moreover, the first speech that Kate delivers upon emerging from the bath indicates that the focus of her sexual desire has indeed switched from men to women. She suddenly shows a decided preference for everything feminine to everything mas-

culine: she loves softness, and deplores hardness and aggressive-
ness ("urgency"):

KATE

The water's very *soft* here. Much *softer* than London. I
always find the water very *hard* in London. That's one reason
I like living in the country. Everything's *softer*. The water,
the light, the shapes, the sounds. There aren't such *edges*
here. . . . I don't care for *harsh lines*. I deplore that kind
of *urgency*. (P. 59; emphasis added)

As the conclusion to his play, Pinter presents one last
symbolic action, which further reinforces the notion that a
reversal of Kate's affection has taken place. He has all three
characters execute an elaborate set of motions which conveys
on three separate levels that Kate has changed sexual partners
and that Deeley has permanently become "odd man out." These
physical movements occur as follows:

ANNA *stands, walks towards the door, stops, her back to
them.*
Silence
DEELEY *starts to sob, very quietly.*
ANNA *stands still.*
ANNA *turns, switches off the lamps, sits on her divan, and
lies down.*
The sobbing stops
Silence
DEELEY *stands. He walks a few paces, looks at both divans.
He goes to* ANNA's *divan, looks down at her. She is still.*
Silence
DEELEY *moves towards the door, stops, his back to them.*
Silence
DEELEY *turns. He goes towards* KATE's *divan. He sits on her
divan, lies across her lap.*
Long silence
DEELEY *very slowly sits up.*

He gets off the divan.
He walks slowly to the armchair.
He sits, slumped.
Silence
Lights up full sharply. Very bright.
DEELEY *in armchair.*
ANNA *lying on divan.*
KATE *sitting on divan.* (Pp. 73–75)

The first implication of this physical movement is related only to the visual image frozen at its conclusion. This image, which also concludes the entire play, is the reverse of that which opens it. The reversal suggests that the dramatic situation which ends the play is antithetical to the one which begins it. First, whereas the play opens with Anna placed in the darkness at the back of the stage, it concludes with her in the light at the front of the stage, Kate's memories having been exposed to the light of consciousness. Secondly, whereas the play begins with Deeley and Kate united by their similar positions while Anna is removed from them, it ends with Anna and Kate tied by their equivalent placements while Deeley is separated from them. Anna, who has taken over Deeley's bed, has probably usurped his role as Kate's lover as well. Deeley, who has just been crying over his loss of Kate, is sitting by himself, the "odd man out."

The second level of meaning, which relates to the entire physical movement, is drawn from a story and its introduction delivered by Anna earlier in the play. Before beginning her anecdote, Anna makes the following prefatory statement:

There are some things one remembers even though they may never have happened. There are things I remember which may never have happened but as I recall them so they take place. (Pp. 31–32)

Anna suggests that although her memories may be of events

that never actually took place, that does not necessarily mean that those events are any less real. If she genuinely believes that they did occur, then for her they are as substantial as any. Furthermore, if she convinces the others that they did occur, then those events are substantial for them as well. Whether or not these incidents actually happened in the past, they do occur in the present ("so they take [present tense] place"), for they are currently lived in the minds of all those who believe her story.

Following this speech, Anna tells her story, the events of which unfold exactly as those in the physical movement that ends the play. The concluding set of motions, then, is a visual concretization of her earlier anecdote.

ANNA

This man crying in our room. One night late I returned and found him sobbing, his hand over his face, sitting in the armchair, all crumpled in the armchair and Katey sitting on the bed with a mug of coffee and no one spoke to me, no one spoke, no one looked up. There was nothing I could do. I undressed and switched out the light and got into my bed, the curtains were thin, the light from the street came in, Katey still, on her bed, the man sobbed, the light came in, it flicked the wall, there was a light breeze, the curtains occasionally shook, there was nothing but sobbing, suddenly it stopped. The man came over to me . . . very slowly, the light was bad, and stopped. He stood in the centre of the room. He looked at us both, at our beds. Then he turned towards me. He approached my bed. He bent down over me. But I would have nothing to do with him, absolutely nothing. . . . But after a while I heard him go out. I heard the front door close, and footsteps in the street, then silence, then the footsteps fade away, and then silence.
Pause
But then sometime later in the night I woke up and looked across the room to her bed and saw two shapes. . . .
He was lying across her lap on her bed. (Pp. 32–33)

The final concretization of Anna's story symbolizes that by the end of the play she has successfully turned her version of the past into a reality. She has convinced the others and herself that her stories are true. Therefore these stories, as represented by the particular one that is enacted, take place in the present in the collective consciousness of all three characters. Anna, having transformed her stories into a reality, has also turned the stories' lesbian implications into a reality. Hence she has "reminded" Kate of the feelings that will permanently draw her to Anna's side.

The third level of meaning arises from one major difference between the final physical movement and Anna's earlier story. There is one incident that takes place at the end of her anecdote that has not yet happened by the conclusion of the set of motions: the man, presumably Deeley, leaves the house on the following morning and is permanently forgotten by the two women.

> ANNA
> But then in the early morning . . . he had gone. . . .
>
> It was as if he had never been. (Pp. 32–33)

We therefore assume that the same action will occur after the curtain has fallen. Deeley, having lost Kate to Anna, will leave the house for good and forever remain the "odd man out." Anna, by having described an incident of the past, will have made that incident occur in the future. Although Deeley's leaving may never have happened, "as she recalls it, so it takes [future tense] place."

Selected Bibliography

WORKS BY CHISTOPHER HAMPTON

When Did You Last See My Mother? London: Faber and Faber, 1967.
Total Eclipse. New York: Samuel French, Inc., 1969.
The Philanthropist. London: Faber and Faber, 1970.
Savages. London: Faber and Faber, 1974.
Treats. London: Faber and Faber, 1976.

WORKS BY HAROLD PINTER

The Homecoming. New York: Grove Press, Inc., 1965, 1966.
The Room & The Dumb Waiter. London: Methuen, 1966.
The Birthday Party. London: Methuen, 1966.
A Slight Ache and Other Plays [*A Night Out, The Dwarfs,* Revue Sketches]. London: Methuen, 1966.
The Collection & The Lover. London: Methuen, 1966.

100

The Caretaker. London: Methuen, 1967.

Tea Party and Other Plays [*The Basement, Night School*]. London: Methuen, 1967.

Lanscape and *Silence* [*Night*]. London: Methuen, 1968.

Old Times. New York: Grove Press, Inc., 1971.

Five Screenplays [*The Servant, The Pumpkin Eater, The Quiller Memorandum, Accident, The Go-Between*]. New York: Grove Press, 1973.

No Man's Land. New York: Grove Press, Inc., 1975.

WORKS BY TOM STOPPARD

Lord Malquist & Mr. Moon. New York: Grove Press, Inc., 1966.

Rosencrantz and Guildenstern Are Dead. New York: Grove Press, Inc., 1967.

Enter a Free Man. New York: Grove Press, Inc., 1975.

The Real Inspector Hound. New York: Grove Press, Inc., 1975.

Albert's Bridge. London: Faber and Faber, 1969.

After Magritte. London: Faber and Faber, 1970.

Artist Descending a Staircase & *Where Are They Now.* London: Faber and Faber, 1973.

Jumpers. New York: Grove Press, Inc., 1975.

Travesties. London: Faber and Faber, 1975.

Dirty Linen. New York: Grove Press, 1976.

WORKS BY OTHER PLAYWRIGHTS

Ayckbourn, Alan. *Absent Friends.* New York: Samuel French, 1975.

Shaffer, Peter. *Equus.* New York: Samuel French, 1973.

Storey, David. *The Contractor.* In *The Changing Room, Home, The Contractor: Three Plays by David Storey.* New York: Avon Books, 1975.

LITERARY CRITICISM

Baker, William, and Tabachnick, Stephen Ely. *Harold Pinter*. Edinburgh: Oliver & Boyd, 1973.

Esslin, Martin. *Pinter: A Study of His Plays*. London: Methuen, 1973.

Ganz, Arthur, ed. *Pinter*. Englewood Cliffs, N.J.: Prentice-Hall, Inc., 1972.

Guernsey, Otis L., Jr., ed. *Best Plays of 1967–1968*. New York: Dodd, Mead & Company, 1968.

————. *Best Plays of 1969–1970*. New York: Dodd, Mead & Company, 1970.

————. *Best Plays of 1970–1971*. New York: Dodd, Mead & Company, 1971.

————. *Best Plays of 1974–1975*. New York: Dodd, Mead, & Company, 1975.

Hayman, Ronald. *Harold Pinter*. London: Heinemann, 1975.

Hinchliffe, Arnold P. *British Theatre 1950–70*. Oxford: Basil Blackwell, 1974.

Ibsen, Henrik. *A Doll's House* (A new version by Christopher Hampton). New York: Samuel French, Inc., 1972.

————. *Hedda Gabler* (A new version by Christopher Hampton). New York: Samuel French, Inc., 1972.

Kerr, Walter. *Harold Pinter*. New York & London: Columbia University Press, 1967.

Lahr, John, and Lahr, Anthea, eds. *A Casebook on Harold Pinter's The Homecoming*. London: Davis-Poynter, 1974.

Molière, Jean Baptiste Poquelin. *Don Juan* (translated by Christopher Hampton). London: Faber and Faber, 1974.

————. *The Misanthrope* (translated by Richard Wilbur). New York: Harcourt Brace Jovanovich, Inc., 1955.

Quigley, Auster E. *The Pinter Problem*. Princeton, N.J.: Princeton University Press, 1975.

Shakespeare, William. *Hamlet*. In *The Complete Signet Classic Shakespeare*. New York: Harcourt Brace Jovanovich, Inc., 1972.

Taylor, John Russell. *Harold Pinter*. Essex: Longmans, Green & Co. LTD., 1969.

NEWSPAPER AND MAGAZINE ARTICLES AND REVIEWS

Esselin, Martin. "Document of Passion." *Plays and Players* (London) 16, no. 2 (November 1968): 18–19.

Gilbert, W. Stephen. "Hampton's Court." *Plays and Players* 20, no. 8 (May 1973): 36–38.

Holmstrom, John. Reviews of *The Philanthropist*. *Plays and Players* 18, no. 1 (October 1970): 32–33.

Reviews of *Old Times*. *New York Theatre Critics' Reviews* 32, no. 24 (1971): 180–83.

Reviews of *The Philanthropist*. *New York Theatre Critics' Reviews* 32, no. 24 (1971): 329–32.

Reviews of *Rosencrantz and Guildenstern Are Dead*. *New York Theatre Critics' Reviews* 28, no. 23 (1967): 254–56.

Taylor, John Russell. "The Road to Dusty Death." *Plays and Players* 14, no. 9 (June 1967): 12–15.

15563